THE ADVENTURES OF ME AND PATRICK

IAN FRY

To the Small Frys – Mollie, Elizabeth & William
To all those whose journeys did not end well and those whose
journeys continue

CONTENTS

PROLOGUE

This is the tale of a poisonous, intense and potentially fatal relationship. A relationship based exclusively on the whims and wishes of one party. It is a story of incessant and unrelenting bullying, oppression, domination and embarrassing taunting, both physiologically and psychologically.

These were the foundations upon which the relationship was built, and they remained the cornerstone of this twisted, dysfunctional union. A union from which, despite an overwhelming desire to do so, it was impossible to escape until a very specific set of unknown events had occurred to enable release from the shackles of the association. It was, both literally and figuratively, the most toxic of relationships.

This very individual, unique and private relationship was played out against a backdrop of intense and invasive treatment and its all-too-familiar effects, as well as the often unseen, unaccountable, distressing, devastating and sometimes laughable consequences of the illness that had brought us together

1

and the medically imposed attempts to ensure I survived the experience.

Despite the overwhelming feelings of helplessness, frustration, desperation and anger that I experienced whilst with Patrick, our time together was not without its lighter moments, and was not devoid of retrospective positivity.

THREE LITTLE WORDS

'You have cancer.'

Three little words none of us ever want to hear. A sentence sure to strike fear to the very core of even the most hardy and resilient soul. It certainly scared the shit out of me.

No other illness commands such a place in the national psyche as cancer does. The 'C' word chills the hearts of almost all of us. According to a survey conducted by Cancer Research UK, cancer is the number one fear of Britons. It found that one in five men and women feared being diagnosed with cancer ahead of debt, knife crime, Alzheimer's disease and losing a job.

Such is society's fear of cancer that friends, family, acquaintances and even medical professionals frequently seemed reluctant to utter the 'C' word when the conversation related to me specifically. It is, in many ways, the illness that shall not speak its name.

During one of my earliest cancer-related appointments, I asked my consultant what the chances were that whatever it was that was going on with my body would be 'something I really don't want.' He knew what I meant. Anyone else present would have known what I meant. Yet neither of us seemed prepared to actually say the word.

'You have cancer.'

For many who are told these shattering words, cancer is so much more than simply a medical condition. It is an avalanche of illness, discomfort, pain, emotions and life-changing events – physical and mental. It is a torrent of frequently bizarre side effects, drugs, tests, scans and hospital appointments that smashes into your life, carrying you and everything about you with it, never stopping or in any way relenting on its inextricable journey to one of two predetermined destinations: death or remission. It consumes everything in its path on the way; everything you know and hold dear; everything that is normal about your everyday life – your preconceptions, your hopes, your present and your future – leaving behind, whatever its final destination, a trail of destruction, chaos, disorder, confusion and physical and mental scarring, not to mention a bucketload of bonus shit.

Having received my diagnosis, I became very conscious of just how little I knew about cancer. I was buried under layers of snow, discovering that I was incredibly poorly equipped for such an expedition. I had no means of escape from my snow-filled burial chamber. I didn't even have a bloody shovel.

Research was the key, I thought. Knowledge is a wonderful thing. Knowledge is power. I would find all the information I could about cancer. That would be my shovel. I would find out what it is and what causes it. I would find out the statistics surrounding cancer, prognoses and mortality rates. I would find out what was going to happen to me and what I could expect to be my new present and future. Yes, that knowledge would be my shovel.

I soon discovered, in these particular circumstances, knowledge was not the all-powerful tool I had anticipated. I didn't find a shovel. What I did find was lots of information about cancer – its causes; the treatment; guidance on how to live with it; advice on how to survive it; what to eat when you have it; what to eat to prevent it; and the stories of individuals and their own very specific journeys and experiences of having or living with cancer – which was all useful to me in their own limited way, each a tiny separate trowel to help with my excavation, but nothing sufficient, either individually or collectively, to dig my way back into the light.

I may have found many trowels, but I didn't find a tool that encompassed all the help, advice and guidance I needed. I soon came to the conclusion that the shovel I sought doesn't actually exist.

I am, therefore, in no way suggesting these pages are the digging implement you will need to escape your own personal avalanche; I do, however, hope they will provide some much-needed assistance and, failing that, at least a distraction.

It is important to stress that this book is not, nor is it intended to be, a guide to dealing with cancer; it is certainly not a manual on how to survive cancer, and it is most definitely not a 'don't worry, think positively, it'll all be okay in the end' self-help-style guide to coping with cancer. It is simply a record of my experiences, which I began recording for cathartic reasons and to give me something to do in my isolation, buried under layers of snow during my own treatment.

Many of my views and experiences will differ from yours and those you know who have been diagnosed with and treated for cancer. The differences in our attitudes and approaches to our respective cancers and treatment simply prove that our journeys are all individual and unique. Just as we are all different, our cancers, our treatments and our experiences are all different.

Having cancer became an all-consuming part of my life and the notes of my adventures grew into far more than simply a diary. They took on a significance of their own while I struggled to find my bearings and dig my own way out towards sunnier horizons.

Although much of the cancer journey is likely to be hideous, my adventures with 'Patrick'– who I will introduce to you in the next chapter – proved that having cancer doesn't have to be all doom and gloom. There will be very surreal moments and some laughs to be had along the way. Experiences of travelling with a cancer are likely to have a significant impact on the life of anyone who undertakes such a journey, and they are not all bad.

I found it incredibly helpful to write about my adventures with Patrick and loved doing so. I hope you will find it enjoyable and perhaps a little helpful.

PATRICK

For me, having cancer, and the struggles I was to face, was never a fight or conflict; it was not me versus my cancer. In order to ensure the process did not become a battle, it helped me to give my cancer an identity, a moniker I could relate to and identify with, someone I could talk to, complain to, blame. Patrick was born.

The idea of naming your cancer may be a rather odd thing to do, but it helped me enormously. Patrick was to be my companion throughout the process. He would be with me every step of the way. This needed to be personal.

Little did I know that Patrick would become so much more than just a label. He took on a personality and identity of his own. He transformed from a mere voice in my head into a visceral manifestation of my illness. He was the life and breath of my cancer, the physical embodiment of my thoughts and fears, my pain and discomfort, and my hopes for the future. It did not take long for this fledgling relationship to take a very sinister twist: Patrick quickly became domineering, controlling and sadistic. He was the evil puppeteer while I dangled helplessly from his strings. I had created my own Frankenstein's monster. His endearing looks belied his wicked character. He was the person/creature/thing for whom the expression 'looks can be deceiving' was created.

The attributing of the name Patrick was by no means a random one. At the time of my diagnosis my daughter Elizabeth (Libby) was in reception, the first year of school. Her class had a mascot, a large cuddly, teddy bear-type of thing, always beautifully adorned in full school uniform. The children loved Patrick. Periodically, in recognition of good work, beautiful behaviour or random acts of kindness, one member of the class would be given the pleasure of taking him home to spend time with their family. I say pleasure... as pleasure for the child concerned it most certainly was. Indeed, it was a cause of huge celebration and something about which the children were to feel very proud. Pleasure for the child; complete pain in the arse for the parents.

Having Patrick come to stay meant he had to be entertained, fed, photographed, drawn, written about and, most importantly, guarded with one's life for fear of losing or in some way disabling him. I was always terrified of becoming the first parent to have to explain to a rather bemused class teacher and an inconsolable group of four- and five-year-olds that I was responsible for the fact that Patrick was no longer his original brown colour, but instead was now brown with white patches following a rather unfortunate incident with a little brother and a paint pot. Far worse was the prospect of being responsible for creating lifelong trauma in this group of small people by returning their much-cherished mascot minus a leg, or, and this was the fear about which parents were known to lose sleep, not returning him at all, Patrick having been lost on a trip, left on a train, or mistakenly put out with the rubbish. None of us wanted to forever be remembered as the parent who killed Patrick.

For this reason, I always dreaded hearing those immortal words from Libby's mouth (and her big sister Mollie's before her) as she came running out of her classroom and leapt into my arms at the end of a Friday afternoon, smiling from ear to ear and declaring: 'I'm so clever! You are going to be SO proud of me! Daddy, I've got Patrick!'

I saw Patrick (the cancer, not the class mascot) as being part of me. Not something, therefore, I particularly wanted to fight with. If he didn't kill me, it wouldn't be because I had beaten him in some epic-style battle in which the hero ultimately prevails, defeating the evil enemy and stands heroically over the vanquished body of his vile opponent. If he didn't kill me, it would be because the drugs had done their job, he didn't get his way, he got bored, gave up and buggered off to take over some other poor sod's life, leaving me in peace to get on with mine.

I was prepared for the journey – albeit a rather lengthy, tortuous, often surreal, frequently uncomfortable and very far from enjoyable one – that Patrick and I were to embark upon. It was to be an adventure that would literally take me away from my normal existence, from the everyday world I inhabited. A world where I did normal everyday things, in a normal everyday way, when I wanted to do them. An adventure that would take me to a new land, to an island where Patrick is king and where I, for the duration of my treatment and my stay on the island, must submit to his wishes.

The Isle of Patrick was in the middle of a river, technically more of an eyot than an island, from where I had an unobstructed view of the lives of everyone else progressing as normal on the banks and the river itself.

From the moment we arrived on the island, it was apparent Patrick had no intention of showing me around, pointing out any amenities that existed, or in any way helping me acclimatise to my new home. Everything was clearly to be done on a 'need-to-know basis', and, evidently, I didn't need to know.

Patrick did show me my accommodation, however, and it was most definitely of the makeshift and make-do variety. In front of us stood (just) a battered, grubby tent. What presumably were once its white canvas sides were now weather beaten and decorated by the faecal contributions of the island's winged occupants. This was very much a previously inhabited tent, a doyen of outdoor accommodation, and I was most definitely not its first occupant. If tents could talk, I suspect this one would have had quite a lot to say.

So much of this situation made me uncomfortable. Patrick wasn't talking much at all. I basically had no idea where I was or how long I was likely to be here for; and now I was being asked, or rather told, to sleep in an old, dilapidated, shit-covered tent.

It wasn't just the disgustingness of the tent that was taxing me. I have always held the view that camping is a frankly ridiculous pastime. Why would anyone choose to sleep outside? No one sees a homeless person sleeping rough on the street and thinks *What a fantastic life they have. I must get myself some of that.* As a species, surely, we have evolved from living outside? Even the most enthusiastic and carefree of tent lovers would baulk at the idea of sleeping in the monstrosity that was to become my living quarters, my Isle of Patrick canvas cell.

Patrick was my personal prison warden, threateningly and ominously standing guard ensuring that the idea of escape was made impossible. The cell itself was filthy. It was hard to get away from the idea of a number of prison cell protests having taken place within its thin walls. The concept of my life being shit was now as much literal as it had been figurative. Now both the internal and external aspects of my life were covered in Patrick-induced shit. The faecal interior lining did serve to provide some protection from the elements, acting as it did as a filler of some of the holes my cell walls were riddled with, and which allowed the wind to whistle around my tiny space and the rain to seep down the walls; but the prospect of spending the next few months in these utterly miserable conditions was as unbearable as it was unfathomable, but my sentence had been delivered by His Honour Judge Patrick and I had no choice but to do my time.

Before I had the chance to try to make myself at home in my squalor, Patrick opened the door (is that what the entrance to a tent is called?) and summoned me outside. Without uttering a word, he gestured for me to exit my cell and follow him. I duly did as I was instructed, and he led me to the nearby shore. There at the edge of a little beach that slid its way into the river stood, albeit somewhat precariously, a wooden sign.

This homemade structure comprised of a wooden stake approximately three feet high, to the top third of which was nailed a flat rectangular board. From the back it was just two pieces of wood attached together. As we made our way onto the sand I could see the front of the sign, the side the passers-by on the riverbank would see. In red-painted letters it read:

ISLE OF PATRICK
POPULATION – 1
KEEP OUT!!!

Below the sign a brush leant casually against a pot of paint. Patrick popped open the lid of the can, dipped the brush carefully into its contents, stood in front of the sign and put a big red 'X' through '1' and wrote '2' next to it. Unless my host was expecting somebody else to turn up, this change in population was reflective of my arrival. I clearly wasn't going anywhere anytime soon.

Patrick walked the short distance to the river, washed his paint brush in the water, returned to join me next to the sign, replaced the lid to the pot and restored both the paint and the brush to the exact positions they had occupied before our arrival. He paused, looked at me, smiled, and without saying a word walked past me and made his way back to the tent.

It was official: I was now, other than Patrick, the only resident of the Isle of Patrick.

I settled in as best I could to my new home and tried to adapt to the demands of my surroundings. I was, at least initially, reluctant to leave the relative security of my disgusting accommodation. I already felt utterly trapped, helpless and alone.

All day every day people passed me along the banks of the river, going about their everyday lives, as I remained marooned and helpless on the Isle of Patrick, each of them blissfully unaware of my perilous and uncertain situation. I would often look out to the passing masses with envy and longing. In envy of their apparently trouble-free, pain-free existence. With longing for the day when I would be able to re-join them in their normality on the mainland – a mainland that was all but inaccessible to me now. It was a normality that surrounded me, goaded me. I wanted normality back. I wanted to be able to take my children to school again; go to the supermarket; climb stairs (in a normal way); sleep (without being constantly reminded of just how useless my body now was and how fragile my existence had become).

How was it that the passers-by I viewed with such jealousy were so blissfully unaware of my predicament? How could it be that their attentions and thoughts were not concentrated on me and my situation? Why did they not have even the slightest inkling of what I was going through? I wanted to put a banner up on the edge of the island for them all to see: 'I have cancer and I'm suffering, please help me'; but such acts of brazen self-pity were strictly forbidden and against the rules on the Isle of Patrick. In truth it wasn't so much a desire for everyone to know about my suffering – I certainly didn't want anyone to feel sorry for me – it was far more a need to be acknowledged and understood. Perhaps a passer-by wearing a T-shirt sporting the slogan 'Patrick is a c*@t' or 'It's all shit. We know'. Anything that recognised the mess I found myself in.

Even if they were aware, even if I was to shout and

plead for help and rescue, there was bugger all anyone could do about it. The Isle of Patrick had a strictly controlled population of two – Patrick and me – and that is how it would stay until this hideous journey concluded in whatever way that may be. Until then it would be an island on which every one of my thoughts and all my actions were overseen, monitored and ultimately controlled by Patrick. This was a dictatorship, an oppressive state. There was nowhere for me to go, even for a short while, where I would feel any sense of inner calm. This was my new home, but I didn't belong here. I felt very alone.

I had been stripped of my citizenship and my passport. Escape from the island was impossible. This was to be my island prison, my Alcatraz, my own 'borderless medical gulag'[1]. There were no guards, no watchtowers or barbed wire fences. There didn't need to be. Departure from the island was to be very much on Patrick's terms. He knew it and I knew it. Any thoughts of escape without his expressed consent were utterly futile.

It was already very evident that the adventures Patrick and I were to share would be far from easy. There would be difficulties along the way, and many times when I would wish above all else that I had never been forced to start the journey in the first place. There would be times when all I wanted was to be back on the mainland, the mainland where I, and not Patrick, was in charge – apart from when my eldest daughter Mollie was in one of her 'I'm seven going on fifteen' moods and it was far from clear who exactly was in charge. But this was a journey borne out of necessity and as such it was one that had to be completed. I saw it simply as a process, a means to an end. A successful journey would, in six months (or thereabouts), equate to remission; a cancer-free, Patrick-free existence and a return to relative normality. A successful journey would enable me to say goodbye to Patrick and depart from the island, but only after I had metaphorically punched him in the face and given him a damn good kicking while he was down to repay him for all the times he had done exactly that to me.

I would leave my captor and swim to the shore – although given my swimming skills and the distinct possibility that I would drown in the process (oh, the irony), perhaps some kind of boat might be more appropriate – departing his island, leaving him far behind and returning to the mainland. My mainland. My normality.

Until that time (hopefully) arrived, Patrick and I would be inseparable. I would become a lovestruck teenager. Patrick would be the last thing I thought about before I went to sleep and the first thing I thought about when I woke up. He controlled my life, what I did and when I did it. It would be Patrick who decided how much my body would hurt on any given day or how sick I would feel. It would be Patrick who dictated when and what I ate on our adventures together. It became rather like being a kid and having six months of your mum packing really crap packed lunches for you every single day, full of stuff you really don't want, and being told 'it's that or nothing'.

Patrick would become the travel rep from hell. The domineering, seemingly tireless organiser who simply cannot be shaken off. The leader who maps out every part of every day. Days crammed full of activities and excursions you really do not want to do. I would be at his whim. Every day I would wake up and ask What has Patrick got planned for me today? What kind of mood will he be in? Will he stop me doing what I want to do? Will he consume every fibre of my body, filling me with pain and discomfort? Will I even know he's there at all? Perhaps he's taken himself off to the far side of the island for some time alone and given me some respite from it all. Wherever he was I knew he would be back. I would make every decision about my life based on Patrick's wishes. He would be responsible for the fact that I couldn't work. It would be because of him that I couldn't be the father I wanted to be to my children. It would be Patrick's responsibility that my body hurt so much of the time. In short, he would control my life to the exclusion of everything and everyone else. He would be the archetypal unwelcome guest; the mother-in-law of travelling companions, but without the ability to babysit the children.

Ultimately, though, regardless of how shit a companion he was and how much I hated his very existence, Patrick was my companion, my partner, my other half.

Patrick would be my shadow. My conjoined twin. For the coming months we would be a pair, a double act. We would become the Chuckle Brothers of the Isle of Patrick. A carcinogenic Ant and Dec. One never without the other. Everything we did, we'd do together.

Despite the hatred I had for my new enforced partner, I consoled myself that many great double acts were not exactly best friends, yet still managed to make their partnership work. Laurel and Hardy didn't always see eye to eye; Simon and Garfunkel had very little time for each other; and Liam and Noel Gallagher would most likely kill each other if left in the same room for too long. I'm not even convinced Ant and Dec's friendship isn't a contrived publicity stunt.

Like all these great pairs, Patrick and I were on this journey together and I was determined we would make our union work the best way possible. Like an old married couple, we would struggle on, for better or worse – or much, much worse. For the duration of our time together, Patrick and I were to be permanent companions. I was to be the Ant to his Dec...or should it be the Dec to his Ant?

Regardless of all the complexities and fundamental difficulties that existed in this most unhealthy of arranged marriages, Patrick and I were in this together. He was MY companion, it was MY cancer, they were MY abnormal cells, it was MY treatment, and it was still (at least for the time being) MY life.

A JOURNEY NOT A BATTLE

One of the MacMillan booklets I read in my efforts to find a shovel stated that 'Cancer is the toughest fight most of us will ever face.' I never saw it like that. At no point either before or during the months of chemotherapy and hideousness did I view what I was doing as a conflict between me and Patrick and those tiny cells that had taken over not only part of my body but, far more significantly, my life. I always thought of it as a journey. A journey that Patrick and I would travel on together, at the end of which, hopefully, we would part company and a new journey could begin for me, alone.

Cancer patients will all have different ways in which they perceive and describe their own cancer. One cancer sufferer described the tumour in his oesophagus as a 'blind, emotionless alien.'[1] Another portrayed her struggles with cancer in this way: 'I'm not fighting cancer…I'm surrendering. To the complete unknown. To the random. To my body. To science. To holy shit there's nothing I can do. To God.'[2]

Another explained how she loathes the word 'journey' when applied to cancer. Her view was that a 'journey implies a pleasant trip to the seaside, a magical mystery tour or an epiphany during some life-changing experience. Cancer isn't a journey. Cancer is a nuclear bomb dropped in the centre of your lovely world, in this case with sod all warning. There's nothing liberating or celebratory or enlightening about it.'[3]

I disagree. My experiences with cancer were absolutely to be a journey – albeit a journey I most definitely did not have a map for. I had no idea how this journey was going to take shape, where I was going, what sights and adventures I was to experience, or the people I would encounter along the way. I was a runaway train, a rudderless ship. This magical mystery tour I was to embark on was just that: a mystery. Yet I thought: *Someone must know how this journey is to progress? How am I going to navigate all the potential hazards that will manifest themselves throughout my journey?*

It soon became clear that there was someone who knew exactly where I was going, what was going to happen to me and what I was to encounter.

Like all those embarking on a journey of any significance I had a travelling companion. Edmund Hillary and Tenzing Norgay climbed together to the top of the world in their ascent of Mount Everest; Captain Scott had Oates as part of his team attempting to reach the South Pole; and Neil Armstrong had Buzz Aldrin to play golf with on the Moon.

Me, I had Patrick.

THE 'C' WORD & ME

I had never given much thought to how I might die. If I had been required to produce a list of ways in which my time might come to an end, aged just forty-three, cancer would have been relatively low down.

A car accident was statistically a possibility; suicide is the biggest killer of men under forty-five (more of that later); and I can think of a few people I've encountered over the years who I would be reluctant to be left alone with for too long for fear of experiencing some serious bodily harm!

I had never drunk to excess; in fact, I'd had a period in my twenties and thirties when I was teetotal. I had never smoked, except passively in pubs, back in the days when smokers were not the social pariahs they are now, huddled together outside in all weathers to enjoy their habit with their select group of fellow lepers. And as a child in my paternal grandparents' house, I spent many hours peering through my grandfather's personal cloud of contamination caused by the smoke from his cigars and pipe. He created a fog so dense it was hard to see my hand in front of my face. A smog unparalleled in the field of human pollution. One akin to those seen over Beijing on a particularly busy industrial production day. My grandfather's emissions would have made even the most prolific, environment-hating Chinese industrialist proud. Given the toxicity of the air I was regularly subjected to until the age of seventeen (when my grandfather died) it's a wonder I made it to adulthood at all.

Adrenalin is not my thing, so meeting my maker as the consequence of a fantastically spectacular but foolhardy act was most unlikely. My sister has always described me as having been a 'rubbish child'. I was never one for climbing trees or undertaking potentially hazardous childhood adventures. I had never therefore succumbed to the usual youthful dangers of falling off or over something or having any spectacular mishap befall me. That rubbishness certainly persisted into adulthood. I had motorcycled to work every day into and through the centre of London, a choice of travel many would regard as exceptionally dangerous, and there were a fair few incidents which could have proved very bad for my health, but with the exception of some scuffed leathers and one broken bike (and ankle) I pretty much got away with it.

I reached the age of thirty without breaking any bones – I had broken my nose twice, once playing rugby as a teenager, the other the result of a playground disagreement, but I don't think that really counts – or having an operation or being hospitalised. I had lived for three decades without being any sort of drain on the NHS. (Although I made up for this in quite spectacular fashion during my time with Patrick.) Ten days after my 'fifteen minutes' (more of that later too) I did manage to achieve all three on one cold January morning, however.

On the way to work my motorbike had an altercation with a patch of black ice. The motorbike lost. This failure of my machine to perform the most rudimental of its functions and remain upright resulted in a broken left ankle and dislocated foot (for me, not the bike). The foot had to be manipulated back into position and the ankle required surgery and the attachment of a four-and-a-half-inch plate to my lower leg, secured by eight sensible-sized screws. In addition, my surgeon decided to add a significantly larger screw to hold the bone together.

This transformation of my leg into some kind of Meccano set was followed in 2012 by my doctor deciding that I could do without my gall bladder. However, two overnight stays in hospital was not a bad return for a man of my age, unless I include the thirty-one hours spent in the maternity ward of our local hospital in London waiting for the first of the Small Frys to be born. In hindsight, I think I preferred the removal of my gall bladder and the attaching of metalwork to waiting for the birth of my first child.

As a relatively fit, healthy forty-three-year-old man, non-smoker, and now only a very occasional drinker, I had never really given cancer a second thought as having any tangible relevance in my life. I was aware of the much-publicised statistical chance of developing cancer at some stage during my life, and, like most people of my age, I had been affected vicariously by cancer. My paternal grandfather had been killed by pancreatic cancer when I was a teenager, and my father died, aged just fifty-eight, as a result of his cancer eleven years before I received my diagnosis.

Despite these second-hand brushes with the Big C, the prospect of having to deal with such an issue myself was still something that simply did not register with me. Whilst I was, as we all are, aware of the tragic stories of children and relatively young people becoming embroiled in their personal struggles with cancer, I still regarded it as something that predominantly affects the elderly, or at least those significantly older than me. My father was regarded as relatively young to have had cancer, and certainly too young for it to have killed him, and I was still fifteen years away from attaining the grand old age of fifty-eight.

Longevity is not a trait my family genes can boast, however. I have spent the whole of my adult life sure in the knowledge I wasn't going to be an attendee at the party of life for terribly long. My taxi was most definitely coming early to collect me. I had always accepted that. I certainly wasn't holding out too much hope of ever receiving a telegram from the Queen. Just being old enough to be given a bus pass and qualifying for a heating allowance is an achievement in my family, but here I was, still in my early forties, and cancer wasn't something that ever appeared on the radar of my consciousness.

If I was to have my own personal encounter with cancer later in my life, as statistically and genetically it seemed more than possible, then I would cross that particular bridge when I came to it. I was blindly anticipating a good few years ahead of me, during which I would watch my children grow up, continue the job I love, and perhaps enjoy other meaningful relationships.

Whilst I was most certainly experiencing other indicators of my advancing middle age – my eyesight was worsening, my hearing wasn't what it was, my waistline was expanding, and I was having to get up in the night far more frequently to pee – cancer was not something I needed to concern myself about. I was much too young for that.

This rather glib, ignorant, ostrich-like approach to cancer and me came to a shuddering, unexpected and most spectacular end shortly after I had finally managed, in a very stereotypically male way, to bite the bullet and make the time to visit my GP about a niggling pressure I had been feeling for some weeks in my throat. I described it as if someone was applying their thumb to my windpipe, just below my Adam's apple.

I saw a doctor I had never met before, who rather disconcertingly looked about fifteen, and who, despite being very charming, came up with a diagnosis that simply did not sound right to me and left me utterly unconvinced. Despite this, I left the surgery having satisfied myself that I had done my bit by making and attending the appointment, armed with a prescription for medication which I never collected, and thought no more about it.

Six weeks later I discovered a not insignificant lump at the base of my neck adjacent to my collarbone. Even the most dyed-in-the-wool, 'I don't need to see a doctor' alpha male, which I am not, would have known this wasn't right and required the opinion of a medical professional. So, for the second time in less than two months, I extremely reluctantly returned to my GP.

This time I was greeted by a doctor who, rather reassuringly, was clearly at least old enough to have actually graduated from medical school. Having explained the history of the 'pressure' on my throat, which was still there, he examined the lump, and although not appearing unduly concerned, and certainly without behaving in any way which caused me to worry, he referred me to an ear, nose and throat (ENT) specialist.

Within a matter of days I arrived at the ENT clinic at my local hospital for my appointment. I was, at this stage, still very relaxed about the whole thing. I had managed to get to my forty-fourth year without ever having much to give me cause to be too frequent a visitor to hospital, at least not as a patient. As a parent visiting A&E with one of my particularly clumsy offspring, yes, but not as a patient.

In ENT, the registrar who examined me was clearly concerned about the lump and booked me in for both CT and MRI scans. In hindsight, the haste with which these appointments were organised should have been the first indicator that something was not quite right. As well as booking the scans I was also given an appointment to see my ENT consultant, Mr Ayshford.

I was still in the realms of blissful ignorance about my condition. It was all frankly rather inconvenient, and I just wanted somebody to deal with it and let me get on with my life without the constant interruption of what were already seeming to be interminable medical appointments, tests and scans.

The following week I had my scans and met Mr

Ayshford for the first time. His manner created an immediate sense of trust and confidence. He was direct, which I like, without ever being dismissive. After examining me, we discussed the findings of the scans and he informed me that the lump would need to be removed for biopsy purposes. He then left the room, only to return to tell me he had booked me in to his own surgical list for the procedure the following week.

I am no expert on NHS procedures and everyday practice, but in my limited experience of hospitals, consultants and the protocol involved in arranging an operation, when a consultant leaves the room and books you in for an operation himself that cannot be a good sign – an example of excellent service certainly, but not good news for me and my imminent diagnosis. I was now beginning to get the distinct impression that things were looking a little less than rosy.

Outside the immediacy of the consulting room and talk of biopsies, I soon found myself, although not forgetting, certainly able to put to the back of my mind any thoughts of impending doom that might have crept briefly into my head during my meeting with Mr Ayshford.

So, in the intervening week, I was not unduly worried. I certainly wasn't losing any sleep or stressing about what came next. However, as the days passed my curiosity levels rose. As most of us do in this age of instant information, I searched the internet in order to find out what this lump might be.

I am always very conscious of the dangers of this type of self-diagnosis, and of believing everything one finds in the masses of information from the vast range of sources available on the world wide web. I therefore restricted myself to what I regarded as trustworthy sites – NHS, MacMillan, etc. – and the information I found was fairly universal in its diagnosis of my condition. I began having ever-increasing doubts about my own invincibility, and I started to question my theory of cancer being the remit almost exclusively of the elderly. Cancer was looking increasingly likely, and it was evident this possibility was what the doctors in ENT were concerned about.

During the course of the relatively short surgery Mr Ayshford removed a swollen lymph node 'bigger than a chicken's egg' from my neck. (Normal lymph nodes are apparently the size of a pea.) After an overnight stay in hospital – what my daughter Libby described as my 'hospital sleepover' – I was sent home and now just had to wait the seven to ten days for the results. Just waiting, in these particular circumstances, is not quite as easy as it sounds. Thousands of people every year experience the feelings associated with waiting for the results of an operation like mine, and I found the whole week rather bizarre.

My mind was a mass of conflicting thoughts and emotions. Part of me was very happy to not return to find out the results, choosing instead to just get on with my life and pretend none of it had ever happened. There was also an element of me that was already feeling enraged by the whole thing – which was, of course, utterly ridiculous, given that the only basis I had for assuming bad news was Dr Google's internet-based diagnosis. Yet I was genuinely angry I was even in this position; and there was, naturally, the pragmatic part of my mind that wanted to find out what was going on, accept it and get on with dealing with it.

After what seemed like an awfully long seven days, I was back at ENT to have my stitches removed. By this time all the conflicting views had been banished from my mind, and I was now desperate to know the results of the biopsy, hoping beyond hope that the only lasting consequence of this whole business would be the three-inch scar that now adorned my neck, and with which my children, particularly Libby, were utterly fascinated. I could then return to my life and place any thoughts of cancer into the 'I don't think about this' box on the shelf of my life.

I am not the most patient of people at the best of times, but the potential magnitude of these results, and the news I had by now convinced myself I was about to receive, meant that I just wanted to know so I could get on with dealing with whatever I was to be told. As Mr Ayshford carefully removed the thread (is that even what stitches are made of these days?) we chatted in the way that doctor and patient do in such circumstances. I don't remember what we talked about, but I'm fairly certain it was pretty banal stuff. The triviality of our conversation was primarily due to the fact that my mind was very much occupied by one, all-consuming question, a question I eventually summoned up the courage to ask: 'Have you received the results of the biopsy?' Completely unfazed by my request, he told me he would check and asked me to wait in the corridor.

I dutifully did as I was told and took a seat outside his consulting room. The usual hustle and bustle of doctors, nurses and patients continued, each rushing past me, all completely absorbed in their own business and utterly oblivious to the plight which was, I was convinced, about to befall me. I distinctly remember feeling very calm, but at the same time knowing there was every possibility, indeed I would have been surprised if he had told me anything else, that I was about to be told I had cancer.

I also recall thinking I was glad I was on my own. The idea of a companion reassuring me that 'Everything is going to be okay' would have been too much for me. I would undoubtedly have snapped back 'How the fuck do you know that!?', or words to that effect. The pressure of having to deal with someone else's views, emotions, thoughts and reassurances would have tipped me over the edge. I was much happier dealing with this situation, my thoughts and the possible consequences on my own. The related consequences of being told that I had cancer started to resonate furiously around my head. Was I going to die? Could it be treated? How would it affect my children? How would it affect me? What about work?

As I sat patiently in my very own waiting room of impending doom, my perceptions of the reality of what having cancer actually meant became all too apparent. Thoughts of cancer equating to death and my own mortality crept to the fore and set up camp in the frontal lobes of my brain.

IAN FRY, A LIFE. WHAT WAS ALL THAT ABOUT?

I became overwhelmingly and uncomfortably preoccupied with thoughts of how little I had achieved in my forty-three years. Somewhat profound and philosophical questions like 'What has it all been for?' and 'Who has benefited from me being here?' began to tax me.

I had always hoped I was someone who offered something to society. I had left my original career as a court clerk at the Old Bailey to train as a primary school teacher, a role I felt would more readily quench my desire to do something I enjoyed whilst at the same time being of some use and benefit to the greater good.

The transition was far from easy. Financially, I swapped my civil service wage for the relative impoverishment of a trainee teacher. The workload was almost cripplingly extensive and constant throughout that training year. Every part of every day had to be planned, analysed and recorded to within an inch of its life.

Anyone who's ever been through teacher training

will understand the ridiculous amount of work involved.

My change in career occurred immediately prior to my second marriage. My first marital union had lasted just over two years before the differences between us became impossible to ignore and the whole thing disintegrated in the most catastrophic and unpleasant way. My union with Mrs Fry #2 lasted considerably longer than my first attempt at this marriage malarkey. Melanie and I were together for eight years before the end came, and, in that time, we were lucky enough to produce our three wonderful children.

Melanie and I have always enjoyed (enjoyed may be overstating it a little) joint custody and care of Mollie, Libby and William, and since our separation, the Small Frys have spent half their time with each of us.

During the time they are with me I am solely responsible for all aspects of their care – washing, cleaning, school runs, homework, bath time, bedtime and all the ad hoc crap that three young children are so adept at coming up with – plus all the usual parenting fun and frolics. I had often heard single parents lamenting how difficult looking after children alone can be. I am ashamed to say I had always felt the difficulties involved were being rather overstated. I soon found out they weren't. Everything you've ever heard about the harshness of raising children alone is true. It's bloody hard, and I only had to do it for fifty percent of the time!

Before the arrival of Patrick, my days were split into two very distinct chunks. The first saw me enjoying the delights of a class-full of other people's children. By the time the evening and the second half of the Fry day came, and the Small Frys and I were back at home, I had been emptied of all the skills, enthusiasm and energy I had utilised all day. Good parenting requires a similar set of skills to those of good teaching – patience, understanding, tolerance and compassion – and just as I have always strived to be the best teacher I possibly can be, being a good father to my babies was immeasurably important. However, by the time I switched from Mr Fry mode to Daddy mode my reserves of parenting were frequently drained to drought levels. If my parenting skills had been water, there would most definitely have been a hosepipe ban imposed. Being a single parent is hard work. The constant demands on my time and my attention as both Mr Fry and Daddy were exhausting.

I had tried to live in as selfless a way as I could. However, the authenticity of that belief was being brought into rather sharp relief now I was faced with the reality and possible finality of having cancer.

I became utterly oblivious to the activity within the rooms and corridors with which I was surrounded and the individuals around me. They were replaced in my head by the most vivid scenario. I envisaged two faceless but rather professional-looking characters standing behind lecterns in a television studio undertaking a prime ministerial candidates-style debate. The live studio audience in front of which they were debating was made up of faces from both my past and present – family, friends, girlfriends, classmates, colleagues, my children – and emblazoned on a large screen behind the participants in the centre of the stage were the words 'Ian Fry, a life. What was that all about?' The debate raged, each of the protagonists vigorously arguing their case. What had Ian Fry's forty-three years of existence been all about? Had they been of any benefit to anyone? Had it all been utterly pointless and something of a waste of time? What would be his legacy? Would he leave a legacy at all?

My thoughts wavered momentarily away from the debate to my son Will, for whom my legacy was sure to include at least one thing. The same as my father's had been to me: hereditary baldness.

Back at the studio, some valid and encouraging points were being made in my favour. I had brought into the world and helped to nurture three intelligent, kind, socially aware young people who would hopefully have their own positive effects on their society. I had given up my previous career to retrain to become a primary school teacher in order to do something useful, a role that would, again hopefully, have made a difference to the lives of at least some of the young people I had taught and guided along the way. I hoped I had made a positive contribution to the lives of some of those I had met, even if only because I had made them smile.

However, the counterargument was being made, equally forcibly, that actually all these things were in fact selfish rather than selfless acts. They were more about self-development and narcissism than kindness and generosity of spirit, and as such merited little credit.

The debate came to an inconclusive end and was replaced in my mind by another equally ridiculous analogy.

I began to imagine life as a football match in which each of us are players within a team: the world around us. It is a game in which we all have to play as a part of that team. A team to which we must all contribute for the group to ultimately be successful. However, within the structure of the team, we can choose to be the archetypal team player, who works tirelessly for the sake of the common good and shared success, or we can be the selfish individual only really interested in achieving self-recognition and glory. During the course of the match, we all experience periods of success where every tackle secures possession of the ball and every shot we take flies into the opposition's goal. Equally, there are other phases of play where each pass we make finds an opponent and we couldn't hit a barn door if our lives depended on it, which in my case it was looking as if it may well do.

I had often thought, not in any morbid or fatalistic kind of way, that if as humans we are indeed in a football match then I did not want to get to the end of my ninety minutes having been a conscientious team player, and played as well as I possibly could, only to find myself lying on my proverbial death bed at the end of the game wondering *What was that all about*? I had of course been working on the assumption that such an introspective internal dialogue would take place once I had at least been given the opportunity to play a full ninety minutes. Now, however, the team manager – nature, luck, God…take your pick – was considering substituting me before the conclusion of the match, and I was still being asked to justify the part I had played in the game. I didn't want to be substituted. I wanted to be allowed to finish the game and have the opportunity to show my real worth and value to the team and the game as a whole over the complete ninety minutes. I didn't want my appearance to be a mere cameo.

RUN, FRY! RUN!

After what I am sure was a relatively short while, although I had lost any sense of time imagining TV debates and metaphorical football matches, a nurse called me into the consulting room. My senses were suddenly heightened to new, painful levels. It was as if someone had turned my sensory dial up to 11. All the sounds of the department to which I had been oblivious prior to this moment suddenly became a cacophony of noise so intrusive it hurt my head. The lights were uncomfortably bright, and I became aware of the very distinctive smell that only hospitals have.

My emotions and sensitivities were also increased. Even the way the nurse – a middle-aged lady of somewhat large proportions, with a very kind face – said, 'Mr Fry, Mr Ayshford will see you now' made me suspicious. Her voice and facial expression radiated comfort and security. However, she smiled a smile that betrayed her inner feelings of commiseration, pity and sympathy. As she opened the door to the consulting room and waited for me to pass her and go in, she placed her hand in the small of my back in a final supportive gesture. All this seemed to happen in slow motion.

As I walked tentatively into the room, Mr Ayshford's desk was, as it had been on all my previous visits, positioned immediately ahead of the door perpendicular to the wall opposite. The patient's chair was in the middle of the room facing the end of the desk. On our previous meetings, Mr Ayshford had sat in his chair in its natural position behind the desk but had turned it through ninety degrees in order to face me. This time, he had moved his chair from behind the desk and positioned it considerably closer to the patient's chair. It had never been in this position before. The nurse shut the door, but remained in the room, and sat down on a chair in the corner, again something that had not happened for any of our previous consultations. She sat much like a prison guard might do for a condemned man, although presumably she was there to act as a surrogate companion in the event I should suddenly feel the need for such support. As the door closed behind me, I turned and looked at her and then glanced back at the door, a door which had literally become a Donald Trump Mexico-style wall separating me from the previous forty-three years and four months of my life. That life had been left behind and was now destined to stay forever in the corridor, stuck permanently in the horrid plastic seats like some rather morbid NHS art installation. Outside the room was my past; inside was my present and future.

Mr Ayshford smiled, like the nurse before him, a kind, genuine smile, but one which was clearly hiding his true feelings, and gestured for me to sit down. As I did, he leaned in towards me. Until that moment there had been a million thoughts smashing around inside my head. Then, without warning, they all suddenly vanished. All except one.

'Escape!' screamed a voice in my head. 'RUN! Go now! Don't have this conversation. Go home and just pretend none of this ever happened. He's going to tell you it's all fine so there's nothing to worry about. RUN! For fuck's sake, Fry, RUN!'

Escape was definitely a possibility. I may not have been the fittest and most spritely forty-three-year-old in the world, but I still fancied my chances of beating my surrogate companion to the door, busting out of there and hotfooting it as far away as possible. When I say as far away as possible, I meant home. Not exactly the greatest place for a fugitive to hide, Mexico it most certainly is not, but it would do for a desperate man in desperate circumstances, and these were now desperate circumstances. I could go home and not have to face this particular music. I could cocoon myself back in my world. A world far away from hospitals, consultants and prison guard nurses. A world where the phrase 'You have cancer' is not permitted. That was where I wanted to be.

Even more important than not sticking around to be given life-changing news, I was absolutely gasping for a decent cup of tea. Hospital tea is crap.

HI, I'M PATRICK

I didn't run. I never got to find out if I could have beaten the nurse to the door. Instead, I stayed, sat in that chair waiting for Mr Ayshford's judgement.

Prior to becoming a teacher I had spent many years working in courtrooms at the Old Bailey and had often wondered what it felt like to be a defendant, standing in the dock waiting for the jury to return its verdict or the judge to pass sentence. As I waited for Mr Ayshford to tell me the results of my biopsy, I was beginning to have some idea, and it was terrifying.

Even before he had said a word, I knew I was in big trouble. So, when he looked me in the eyes and said, 'I'm afraid it's not good news' it came as absolutely no surprise. It was followed by those three immortal words: 'You have cancer.' The diagnosis was Stage III Hodgkin's lymphoma: cancer of the lymphatic system.

Although he must have delivered this kind of news hundreds of times to hundreds of different patients, what he said seemed not in the least rehearsed, and the way he said it resonated with genuine sympathy.

Although some further conversation took place, as hard as I tried, I failed spectacularly in taking any of it in. All I heard was 'You have cancer.' After that I heard nothing.

At the end of our very one-sided conversation, there were a few seconds of contemplation, during which nothing further was said by anyone. I shook Mr Ayshford by the hand and thanked him and the nurse, who had sat silently in the corner of the room while my life was changed, and walked back into the corridor.

The sounds, smells and sights of the clinic had changed again. I was now surrounded by muffled, indiscernible noise and was oblivious to the odours and colours that greeted me. I walked out through the waiting room utterly unaware of anything or anyone around me. Amanda Holden, Lucy Verasamy, Kate Beckinsale and Michelle Keegan could have all been in that waiting room, scantily clad, surrounded by balloons and wearing neon signs saying 'Fry, I'm here for you', and I wouldn't have noticed. (I decided not to include the Duchess of Cambridge in this list, fearing it a little disrespectful, not to mention treasonous to include our future queen in such a thought process.) The greatest rock bands of all time – Status Quo, AC/DC or Iron Maiden – could have been playing in the corner and I wouldn't have batted an eyelid.

One often hears of people describing such experiences as being 'out of body'; in other words, they seem to separate their mental and physical selves and are able to observe matters from afar.

For me it felt exactly the opposite.

What I was feeling was a wholly introspective, internal experience. It was as if all my emotions, feelings and senses had been sucked deep inside my body. I had absolutely no concept of what was happening around me.

I made my way back to my car in something of a trance, presumably paying for a parking ticket on the way, and drove home. The journey back to my house took only a matter of minutes, but I remember getting home and having absolutely no recollection of how I got there. I sat on my sofa, surrounded by an almost oppressive silence, trying to digest what had just happened to me. I knew from what I had read and what Mr Ayshford had just told me, at least the bits I could remember, that there was now to be a course of treatment, but at this stage I had no idea what that really entailed. It was one of those occasions when ignorance could be likened to bliss; but it was more of a black hole of nothingness for me.

I assume it is always difficult to remember how one feels in that relatively small period of time immediately after being told one has cancer. Undoubtedly, there were myriads of questions, and much confusion dominating my thought processes; however, I do remember feeling one overriding emotion. The reason I remember is that I vividly recall how strange it felt that this should be how I was reacting to the news Mr Ayshford had given me. I felt incredibly calm.

It felt wrong to feel this way. Surely, I should be awash with emotion? I had just been told I had cancer. I should be feeling something?

'What is wrong with you, Fry?' I heard a voice ask. 'No one responds to being told they have cancer like this!'

So confused was I by the presence of this voice that I

momentarily glanced around the room to locate the speaker, knowing full well there was no one else in the house.

'Hi. I'm Patrick,' the voice continued. 'I'm your new companion. It'll be just you and me from now on. We're going to have a great time together.'

Patrick? I thought. The only Patrick I knew was Libby's class mascot; that infernal bear no one wanted to be responsible for losing.

'Welcome to the club,' Patrick said.

Club? I thought. *What club*? I wasn't yet sure exactly what club it was I had apparently inadvertently enrolled in, but I was already pretty sure it was not an organisation I wanted to be part of. I would be needing to scan the small print to look for the cancellation clause.

'Welcome to the Cancer Club,' Patrick said, persisting with his welcome speech.

Cancer Club? Yep, this was most definitely not a club I wanted to join. *Who do I speak to about cancelling my membership*? I thought.

'The Cancer Club. You'll love it. No getting out of it now. You're already a fully paid-up member.'

I scoured the paperwork for a means of escape, but Patrick was right. There was no getting out of it. I was in. And membership of the Cancer Club dictated that, henceforth, Patrick would always be with me, both physically and aurally. Always resplendent in his school uniform, he would walk by my side, accompany me to all my appointments, securely belted into the passenger seat of my car for our expeditions to some of the more far-flung medical establishments in the West Midlands, and provide a

44

running commentary on every aspect of our journey together.

Hearing a voice from an imaginary source was a new experience for me. I've had my difficulties with mental illness but, even for me, hearing voices was a new one. It would, however, become a recurring theme over the coming months; one that would soon establish itself as an inherent part of my life. And the fact that he was a bear – *the bear* – well, what was that all about?

This first meeting was more than a little uncomfortable. I didn't know what to say or do. Should I answer him? Was I supposed to enter into a conversation with this voice in my head? What are the social expectations in this rather bizarre situation? I had no frame of reference. Nobody does. I don't suppose even Debrett's has a chapter called 'How to navigate your first encounter with a voice in your head'. I had no idea what to do. Perhaps if I ignored it, it would go away. I had just met this new person/thing in my life. I was utterly clueless and literally lost for words. This was very quickly becoming the worst and most awkward blind date ever.

I managed to momentarily push aside the fact that I was hearing voices, the awkwardness of the resulting silence, my membership of undoubtedly the worst club in the world, and my apparent acquisition of a new companion – a bear called Patrick – and redirected my focus to the rather more pressing issue at hand.

Even more disconcerting than the new levels of crazy I had now reached was the fact I felt no sense of panic or anger, fear or despair about the news Mr Ayshford had given me. There were no tears. No sense of frustration. There were no thoughts of trepidation for the difficulties and the struggles ahead. There was a moment of reflection and silence while I contemplated this somewhat puzzling state of affairs, this numbness, this calm. I felt nothing.

'Don't worry,' Patrick whispered. 'You will.'

WHAT NEXT?

I sat in my lounge, looking at but not seeing the artwork and the pictures of my children on the walls, desperately attempting to order my thoughts in a way that would enable me to begin to process them, whilst also trying to put aside the fact I was now hearing voices – or a voice. I began to wonder what might happen next. I did not have even the slightest idea.

It felt rather like the day my ex-wife Melanie and I brought our first daughter, Mollie, home from hospital. Having secured her in her car seat with the care one might handle a Ming dynasty vase, and driven back to our family house at the speed of a funeral procession, we arrived home. The car seat was removed with such care that an observer would be forgiven for thinking it was somehow booby trapped. I walked into the house in a way I had never walked before, clutching the car seat and my thirty-six-hour-old progeny with such focus and concentration that every step was taken as though walking on glass.

Once in the house I placed the car seat on the lounge

floor, with Mollie still securely strapped in. Melanie and I sat on the sofa in front of her. We looked at our beautiful baby and then at each other, both thinking exactly the same thing: What happens now?

In the same way that no one really prepares you for the first moments spent at home with your first child, nothing can prepare you for what you do when you get home after being told you have cancer.

The fact that I was alone was again, perhaps strangely, quite comforting. If someone had been there with me, I am sure there would have been an awkwardness to any conversation while we both tried to second guess the other in terms of how much, if at all, they wanted to discuss what had just happened. It did feel a little odd having such tumultuous news and nobody to tell, but I didn't have anyone I felt the need to share it with immediately.

Years before I embarked on this new chapter in my life with Patrick, I had been diagnosed with a personality disorder. The term 'personality disorder' is frequently associated with anti-social, irrational and/or erratic behaviour; it was certainly one I had regularly heard used in court to in some way excuse the behaviour of defendants who were being tried or had already been found guilty of some pretty heinous stuff. To have such a term attributed to me was most definitely disturbing.

My disorder is not particularly hardcore in the scale of such ailments, and most certainly could not be used as an explanation or excuse for any reprehensible behaviour on my part. Mine is categorised by psychiatrists as a 'suspicious' disorder, which I assume is a description of the symptoms rather than the validity of the disorder itself. It is characterised by a lack of interest in social relationships, a tendency towards a solitary or sheltered lifestyle, secretiveness, emotional coldness, detachment and apathy.

Whilst I do not believe all those characteristics are strictly applicable to me, one consequence of my condition is the absence of any close relationships as it is common for sufferers of this disorder to have few or no close friends. This is most definitely true of me.

I spent years having regular sessions with a psychologist. She once told me I should prepare myself for the fact that once my children had left home, I would end up living life as a hermit. I didn't challenge her view. I wasn't unhappy with the summation.

Despite not having anyone close enough to me to necessitate sharing my news immediately, there would, of course, be people I would need to tell in due course. As the family member to whom I am closest, I would tell my sister Amanda. My headteacher would have to be told and, as the mother of my children, Melanie would also need to know. My diagnosis was clearly going to impact on each of them, albeit in very different, as yet unidentified ways, but none of them needed to know right now. Waiting a couple of days would not make any difference to anyone. So until I decided to share my news it would remain my little secret (bloody huge secret, more like). I was happy being alone with my thoughts, such as they were. And Patrick, apparently, my new constant companion, the latest addition to my life.

'So, I got you,' Patrick chimed, sounding more than a little pleased with himself. 'I bet you're thinking *Why me? I know I would be.'*

I was still rather nervous and somewhat unsure about how I should deal with this abomination that had set up camp in my head. I didn't respond verbally, but his question did strike a chord: he wasn't wrong. Thoughts of 'Why me?' had certainly flirted momentarily with my consciousness. I think it is only natural to ask such a question in any situation where an event occurs that statistically shouldn't happen to you, but nevertheless comes banging on the door of your life, demanding to be let in and proving more difficult to get rid of than a persistent Jehovah's Witness.

I like a little flutter now and again, and would certainly have been prepared to stake a decent amount of my hard-earned on the fact that I would not get cancer when I was forty-three. So the question of 'Why me?' did tax me, but it was not a question I pondered for very long. The answer to this particular quandary was immediately blindingly obvious and very simple. Why not me?

Regardless of why this had happened to me, and where I now found myself, what came next, and who the fuck Patrick was, there was one thing I needed to do as a matter of urgency…that most British of responses to any sort of crisis or emotional upheaval. I put the kettle on.

MY CANCER DAY

What I had not fully appreciated at the time was that in the seconds it had taken Mr Ayshford to deliver his findings, my life had changed irrevocably. Although the nature of the changes was, and to a large extent remain, inconclusive, one thing was certain: nothing about me or my life was ever going to be the same again. In both the short and longer term everything about me was going to be different. In the longer term, if there was to be one at all, my attitudes toward life – my life, the lives of my children and the views I hold of others – were to be changed forever.

What I very soon began to realise was that for the immediate future – the as yet undefined time any treatment I was to receive would take – nothing about this change was going to be good. It was going to be one massive crock of shit into which I would have to immerse myself on a daily basis in order to then have merely a chance of being told that the cancer had gone. If I got to that stage, and apparently there was a 'good' chance I would, I would then be faced with the realisation that as a 'cancer survivor' I would spend the rest of my life without the treatment and the scans and the crap cells, but a life of psychological damage filled with paranoia, the cancerous sword of Damocles hanging over me, knowing that if the cancer returned I would be in real trouble and it would most likely mean the end of my particular journey once and for all.

However, that was all for the future. The reality of the here and now was I had cancer. It was 30th May. My Cancer Day. Shit Patrick's Day. The day that Patrick officially became a part of my life. A parasitic, energy-sapping appendage that had clamped itself onto me and clearly intended to stick around for the duration. He was making himself comfortable sprawled out on the sofa of my life, television on, remote control commandeered, bottle of beer in one hand, family size bag of Doritos in the other. He wasn't going anywhere.

I was now riding the Cancer Express with Patrick as my permanent travelling companion. We were travelling at high speed with the tickets Patrick had purchased for us on our one-way trip from Normality to a destination as yet undecided, possibly Death, maybe Remission, calling at Painsville, Chemo Junction, Fatigue Town and every stop in between.

While I sat firmly glued to my seat, incapacitated by the fear and anxiety that had now put in an appearance, Patrick sat opposite me munching through the vast range of tasty snacks and sipping refreshing beverages he had accumulated during his numerous visits to the buffet car. He loved nothing more than to flaunt some of my favourite culinary pleasures in front of me, knowing full well I was unable to partake because of the constant nausea and the damage he was doing to my mouth and my digestive system.

Patrick was one of those travellers who had scant regard for his fellow passengers. An irritating tosser, he was completely oblivious to the feelings of the other customers; music playing through his headphones at a volume that allowed it to be heard, but the tune and lyrics indiscernible, creating a muffled, mind-numbingly frustrating rhythmical white noise so infuriating it creates one of two, equally socially inappropriate, responses: asking him to turn the volume up so we can listen properly, or snatching the earphones from his ears and whipping him with them. This musical torment was only interrupted briefly during the journey in order for him to conduct a telephone conversation at such a volume that the whole carriage was made unwillingly party to a tête-à-tête so banal that sticking knitting needles in my ears would have been a preferable option to listening to his views on the previous evening's episode of Love Island, the outcome of his mum's latest doctor's appointment about her haemorrhoids, or his views on the up-to-the-minute celebrity gossip posted on Instagram.

The carriage was surprisingly busy. A large number of other passengers sat, as I did, accompanied by their own menacing-looking companion. So crowded was it that the Cancer Express took me back to those innumerable hideous commutes to and from the Old Bailey, crammed into utterly miserable conditions with other commuters all enduring the same sorry experience, all as miserable as each other, wishing more than anything else that they were somewhere, almost anywhere, else. However, like the daily commute our journey on the Cancer Express was a matter of duress not choice.

Daily travels on the Underground was a part of London life I most certainly did not miss, but at that particular moment with Patrick I would happily have relived all those hideous journeys on the tube if it meant being able to alight from the Cancer Express and rid myself of him. Unfortunately, getting off the train before our designated stop was not an option. Make yourself comfy, Fry, and pass me the knitting needles!

One significant difference between my newest form of public transport and that which I had left behind in London was the levels of communication permitted between passengers other than your allocated companion. In my hometown, one I shared with over nine million people, commuters in their hundreds of thousands make their way into and across our capital city on their daily commute. Despite this most unique of British shared experiences, any form of communication is, by decree of the sternest of unwritten laws of the capital, strictly prohibited. Uttering a single word and any form of non-verbal interaction, even with a fellow traveller so close to you you can feel their breath on you, is the gravest breach of this London social convention. However, Patrick, our fellow passengers on the Cancer Express and I, were not in London. Consequently, experiences, thoughts and fears were openly exchanged.

Although we were all travelling in the same direction, each of us was travelling our own very individual journey, each armed with a different ticket, the destination of which was known only to our own given companion.

Unlike any other train on the British railway system, the Cancer Express always ran to time, unerring in its punctuality, each station visited at exactly its scheduled day and hour. Many of the train's incumbents avoided the wonders of some of the stops en route and remained on the train. Some were pressganged into alighting at each and every stop. We departed only temporarily to enjoy the local hospitality, before rejoining the assembled masses on board as we all made our way along the line of despair to the next stop. Whatever the specifics of our individual journeys, we all shared the same wish: to avoid pulling into Terminal Terminus. We were each hoping we actually held the golden ticket – a return to Normality.

I HATE LOSING

One of the things we are commonly told about cancer and an individual's struggle with their own illness is that it is or has been a 'fight' or a 'battle'. Newspapers frequently print headlines screaming how an individual had endured, but lost, a 'battle against cancer'. I was regularly told by those I met in the street, or who messaged me, 'you can beat this' or 'you will win this battle', whilst others extolled the need for me to 'keep fighting'.

It appears to be a generally accepted view, at least amongst commentators, that cancer is something sufferers have to fight and that the battle against the illness is ultimately won or lost…a view, it would appear, not universally held by those who have actually suffered at the hands of this vile foe.

A report published years after Patrick and I were introduced indicated that whilst there were those with their own Patrick who regarded such terms as empowering – for them they engendered thoughts of a challenge to be won – the preference was for more 'clear, factual language'. Many cancer sufferers regard terms such as 'fighter', 'warrior' and 'hero' as inappropriate rather than uplifting.[1] The use of the terms 'war' or 'battle' were also unpopular amongst some who have or have had cancer. One participant explained how she wanted to be described as someone 'living with incurable cancer'.

I read one description of cancer sufferers as 'generations of men and women who have waged a battle against cancer [...] one in which the adversary is formless, timeless, and pervasive [...] there are victories and losses, campaigns upon campaigns, heroes and hubris, survival and resilience and inevitably, the wounded, the condemned, the forgotten, the dead.'[2]

This is the terminology that has become de rigueur when describing cancer and the associated struggle. It is the socially accepted norm that anyone with cancer must 'fight' their 'battle'. It is almost as if the use of the word cancer in relation to an individual must be accompanied by some reference to a conflict; it has become part of society's subconscious. Cancer = battle or fight.

Cancer sufferers are not exempt from this cultural conditioning. So, when we are given those three little words, we are expected to immediately gird our loins, fall into battle formation, artillery at the ready, to fight off our faceless enemy.

Use of the term 'battle' suggests a contest, a fight, a race, whatever kind of competition one wishes to liken it to, and any competition is naturally resolved with there being a winner and a loser.

If my association with Patrick was a 'battle' then, ultimately, one of us would win. A victory for Patrick would be intolerable, on so many levels. I hate losing. I wasn't mad about the prospect of dying either.

The only thing I hate more than losing is not being good at something. Given I had no way of knowing just how adept I would be at this fighting cancer malarkey, it seemed rather churlish, as a novice, to take on such a veteran. Patrick was the undisputed champion. If it wasn't a battle, then I couldn't lose. If the outcome for me was to be an unfavourable one, at least I could take some solace from the fact I hadn't been beaten.

I didn't want to feel I had somehow failed. I didn't want to have fought and lost. I wanted to avoid adding 'failure' to my epitaph. I didn't want my children to have to deal with the notion I had failed them in not winning the fight. I didn't want to feel, nor did I want the Small Frys to feel, that the outcome could have been different if only I'd fought harder, given more of myself to defeating Patrick, just applied myself a little better. I didn't want anyone to think I didn't want it enough. I really, really did.

If you fight cancer in the way almost everyone (most of whom have not had cancer) implores a sufferer to do and things do not end well for you, that equates to losing, being beaten, defeat, failure. You tried, you fought, you battled. You failed.

As if the prospect of ending your life as a failure were not enough, the societal pressure extolling the virtue of cancer patients to 'fight' their own Patrick causes a huge amount of daily emotional turmoil. My friends, family and acquaintances often used very well-intentioned but nevertheless clichéd phrases, which served only to create extra pressure and mental angst for me. Encouraging me to 'keep fighting' or to 'stay strong' made those days when the last thing I wanted to do was fight or be strong even more difficult.

There were many days when all I wanted to do was curl up in a ball, even though my body was not physically capable of contorting itself into any such position, and to give up. I wanted to be allowed to have those days and those feelings, and to do so without the guilt of believing I had somehow let down those who exalted such efforts from me because I was not 'fighting' or being 'strong'.

I needed to be able to have days when I could submit obligingly to Patrick's will. To listen to what he was telling me about what I could and couldn't do and be permitted to feel weak, because that was how I felt.

Those providing support, and cancer sufferers themselves, try so hard to always get it right, often to the point we are so afraid of getting it wrong, we end up saying nothing at all in order to prevent such a disaster. We must accept there will be days and occasions when certain descriptions of the cancer, how the sufferer is feeling or how they should approach their illness and treatment, are just inappropriate and excruciatingly unhelpful. If we all accept that then we have a chance of opening a much more honest dialogue about our own illness.

We need to remove the trepidation and stress involved in communicating about cancer and its treatments.

I saw a TV ad for Cancer Research's 'Race for Life'. It had the rather aggressive strap line: 'Up Yours, Cancer'.

I also saw an advert on the tube in London, also for the 'Race for Life', that read:

'OI, CANCER! Want to know what all the people in this carriage have in common? None of them like you. You're more hated than the guy who stops the doors from closing, the girl whose headphones are constantly going bmmmm-tssssst, bmmmm-tssssst, or the muppet who doesn't get out of his seat for a pregnant lady. But guess what, cancer?'

As a society our approach, led by those who work with and against cancer, to facing the challenges of cancer can be very aggressive. I never saw it that way.

NOTHING ABOUT THIS IS 'GOOD'

As the days passed following Mr Ayshford's uttering of those never-to-be-forgotten words of doom, some of the details of our subsequent conversation began to come back to me. Hugely significant parts of our discussion that had been archived in the 'you don't need this stuff now' folder in my head, filed completely arbitrarily amongst other bits of information I assumed I would not need again any time soon, alongside such once important but now long-forgotten facts – how to calculate the area of a circle; asking for directions to the library in French; the names of all seven of Snow White's dwarves – Mr Ayshford's words were starting to creep back into my consciousness.

Having informed me in a very calm, empathetic and measured way that the biopsy performed on the mass he had removed from my neck just seven days earlier confirmed I had cancer, Mr Ayshford then went on to put this information into a little more context.

'Your prognosis is good, Ian,' he said. Evidently in an attempt to reassure me.

'What does that mean?' I asked. I was prepared for the fact that our definitions of the word 'good' may be more than a little different.

'There is only a thirty percent chance your cancer will kill you,' came the rather surprisingly, evidently not very good response.

'Only!?'

'Hodgkin's lymphoma is a 'good' cancer to have,' Mr Ayshford continued, in his attempts to assure me. 'One of the top five.'

Lucky me, I thought. So, I had the Tottenham or Chelsea of cancers: good but not the best. It could have been worse; I could have had the West Ham of malignancies: never the best and always in serious danger of getting relegated.

Such positivity delivered by those in the know is, for a very short time, uplifting, and a welcome distraction from the mass of negativity that immediately consumes one's thoughts when put in this situation, which is presumably the desired intention. However, even a little scratching away at the surface of Mr Ayshford's definition of 'good' very quickly revealed a far less positive reality. I was obviously pleased to have received this 'positive' news, knowing that it could, of course, have been far, far worse. However, confronted with the very relative nature of the term 'good' in this context, a very different conclusion can be reached, making the whole situation feel significantly less positive.

Can there be any other situation in life where a course of events upon which you are about to embark, where the survival rate is only seven out of ten, would be regarded as 'good'?

Whilst I completely understand the doctors' and others' use of the word 'good', I felt it was important to be clear in my own head about this and contextualise it all a little better. NOTHING about having any cancer, even a good one, is good. It is all merely relative forms of shit. The disease is shit, the treatment is shit, the physical and emotional effects involved are shit. The impact on your life and those close to you is shit, and you endure all that simply to have a chance it doesn't kill you.

Even with a good cancer the survival rates are not good, they're simply less shit than with other cancers. I had been given a prognosis that I had a seventy percent chance of surviving my cancer, which still left a thirty percent chance that I wouldn't.

The next time you are in a room with nine other people, imagine being told that as a result of something you had no control over, and had done nothing to elicit, only seven of you will still be alive in a year's time. Would anyone regard that as being good odds? You also have to bear in mind that, statistics aside, there are no guarantees. You may well get through all the shit that comes with treatment, only to be told it's going to kill you anyway.

None of this is good; but that isn't to say it couldn't be worse. I have always been acutely aware that my situation could have been a whole lot worse, and I was extremely lucky compared to many, many others. However, regarding something as being good simply because it could have been considerably worse is something of a paradox. When people, whether they were medical professionals or not, referred to my cancer as being 'good' they were presumably attempting to put a positive spin on what was otherwise an utterly shit situation. Such positivity is, I am sure, important for some, and will undoubtedly be of benefit and bring some comfort to others. In my case it was a way of them reminding me it could have been worse and that my chances of survival were relatively good. In short, by expounding such positivity in relation to a wholly negative situation, about which there are no positives, what people were actually doing, albeit inadvertently, was reducing my freedom to be angry/upset/pissed off. They were denying me the opportunity to think and articulate my feelings that actually nothing about the situation I found myself in was good. It was ALL SHIT.

Instinctively none of us, including me, at least for a short while, want to be seen to be flying against such a consensus of positivity. I allowed myself to be swept along on a wave of optimistic thought and an attitude of 'it will all be okay'. Swimming against such a strong tide of positivity was incredibly difficult; and allowing myself to ride the waves of hopefulness and optimism in this way was to deny to myself and those around me the very stark reality of the situation. The emphasis on positive thought became a deluge. Instead of sweeping me along I began to drown, submerged under the pressure of constant encouragement to remain positive. I didn't feel like being positive. It felt like I had very little to be positive about. But now I was being hampered in my freedom to feel the way I wanted and, more importantly, needed to feel about my situation.

The bottom line is, how ever you want to stack it, however positive you want to be, or how much you try to put a positive slant on it, one thing is undeniably true: the whole thing – the diagnosis, the treatment, the side effects, the prognosis, the after effects, the emotional turmoil, in fact everything that comes with a relationship with Patrick – is a crock of shit. Describing any part of having cancer and its related processes as good is rather like telling an amputee that it's good they now only have one leg, because they can now save money on shoes, or qualify for a blue badge…and nobody would ever do that. So why do we feel the compulsion to do it with cancer patients?

WE'RE GOING TO BLAST IT

My care was now passed to those Mr Ayshford described as the 'clever doctors'.

A week after Shit Patrick's Day, I made my first visit to Rowan Suite, the haematology clinic at Worcester Royal Hospital. The word 'suite' always conjures up images of vast exclusive hotel rooms, beautifully decorated and furnished, chock to the brim with every conceivable amenity one could wish for and a balcony affording amazing vistas into the distance and to the world many storeys below. Rowan Suite was most definitely not that kind of suite.

I booked in at reception, took a seat and sat patiently waiting for my name to be called.

I am accustomed, as are all British adults, to the etiquette of the doctor's/hospital waiting room. The level of expectation in these rooms is such an intrinsic part of British life I'm amazed that 'how to behave in a doctor's waiting room' does not form part of the national curriculum taught to primary school children alongside 'stranger danger' and the perils of smoking.

Perhaps I should start teaching it in my PSHE lessons, and get the children to make posters that could be distributed to the local surgeries and hospitals and displayed in their waiting areas to ensure all patients are aware of, and comply, with these cultural expectations. I imagine the posters would read something like this:

WAITING ROOM RULES

Rule #1
DO NOT
make eye contact with any of the other waitees.

Rule #2
NEVER
sit next to someone else unless ALL other
seats are taken.
(Sit as far away from other waitees
as humanely possible.)

Rule #3
DO NOT
attempt to engage in idle chit-chat with
any other waitees.
(Any breach of Rule #3 will result in being
branded a 'nutter'.)

Rule #4
EXPECT
the receptionist to be unnecessarily loud when talking
to patients, and for your personal details – name, date
of birth, address and the reason for your appointment

– to be discussed openly without any form of discretion.

Rule #5
YOU WILL
have to wait.
(Appointments run to time only in the most exceptional of circumstances.)

I knew the rules. I had always complied with them before and today was no different. Yet despite the comfort I felt sitting in a room where such restrictions existed, the familiarity of the setting and the situation I was in, I felt utterly lost. The lack of awareness and understanding about what was going to happen to me was disarmingly uncomfortable.

Patrick appeared for the first time that day.

'Morning. You look worried,' he said.

We were still at the stage of our relationship where our conversations were one way. He talked. I said nothing. I certainly wasn't going to venture into the bizarre world of having a conversation with a figment of my imagination for the first time in a public place. That would be a spectacular breach of unwritten rule #6: Do not talk to yourself!

'I love this bit,' he continued, not at all relenting in his determination to be the spokesperson for everything to do with my cancer, nor put off by the fact I had never actually replied to him. He climbed onto the chair next to mine and shuffled himself back in the seat. He seemed very content to chat away, enjoying the sound of his own voice and his domination of our situation. 'It's so new. So fresh and exciting. The uncertainty of how things are going to work out, whether we have a future.'

Although we clearly had very different views about what constituted 'exciting', he was certainly right about one thing: neither of us knew what the future held for us and where this relationship was going.

I was already feeling anxious as I sat waiting. My feelings of unease had definitely not been helped by the appearance of my fledgling companion and the uncertainty this new relationship engendered within me.

Anyone who really knows me would most certainly describe me as a control freak. I struggle with any situation over which I do not have full control. I am never comfortable not knowing what to expect. I hate surprises at the best of times. I don't enjoy unexpected presents or trips even when, as they invariably do, they turn out to be wonderfully thought out and pleasurable. For someone who finds even these kinds of surprises a cause for discomfort, sitting waiting in complete ignorance of what was about to happen to me was uncomfortable in the extreme. This whole cancer business was way out of my control.

I have absolutely no idea how long I waited for my name to be called, but when it was, I dutifully followed the doctor into a small consulting room, remarkable only in how unremarkable it was. The young male doctor shook me by the hand and introduced himself. He was charming, but more than slightly eccentric both in appearance and manner. He was terribly well spoken, but rather bumbling, like a young Boris Johnson only with slightly less ridiculous hair.

Small talk was exchanged before we moved on to

the rather more pressing issue at hand, but despite being very affable he was not able to answer a number of my questions and seemed unaware of how exactly my treatment would progress.

'Who is this fella?' Patrick asked rather scathingly. 'I'm glad he's not looking after me. He's definitely having some arse/elbow differentiation problems.' He chuckled. I had not heard him laugh before, but it was certainly not the last time he would openly enjoy our experiences on our journey together. Enjoying himself he most certainly was.

Patrick's intervention had momentarily distracted me from my conversation with the doctor. I was now back in the room, and the doctor's inability to answer what I regarded as the most basic of questions was starting to rankle, to say the least. My levels of angst were now reaching atmospheric proportions as I sat and listened to this blathering idiot. There was a clear correlation between my levels of anxiety and the desperation with which he was floundering around in his increasingly frantic attempts to address the issues I was raising. I was not in the mood for such indecision. I wanted answers, information, guidance and, most importantly, to feel that the doctors whose care I was now under, and who were to take me through the most important phase of my life to date, knew what they were doing. I wanted my shovel!

Faced with this apparent lack of knowledge and direction, my feelings of anger and agitation soared. Intolerance was rapidly becoming my overriding sensation. It finally became too much. I demanded to speak to someone else; someone who could tell me what I needed to know. So difficult and uncomfortable had I made the situation for the doctor that I got the distinct impression he was rather pleased to be provided with an excuse to leave the room in search of a colleague he could pass me on to, relieved to make me someone else's problem.

Patrick chirped up again. 'That was a bit harsh. He was only trying to help.'

The honeymoon period, if indeed there ever was one, had already come crashing to an end for me and Patrick. I wanted more than anything to tell him to fuck off, but I remained acutely aware of the fact I was being spoken to by an apparition, and responding to him would be to acknowledge and accept his existence. I was also conscious that I had no way of knowing who might be able to hear me, so I decided restraint would be the better course. Apart from anything else, I didn't need the medical staff to add 'prone to unexplained outbursts – Tourette's??' to my medical notes.

I am still embarrassed about the way I behaved that day toward the doctor. I put him in an unenviable and very difficult position. I have often thought I would like to apologise to him, but unfortunately never had the chance. I never saw him again. Not even in passing during my numerous visits to the clinic over the coming months.

Having resisted the temptation to tell Patrick to do one, the doctor's place in the room and the Fry firing line was taken by Dr Fiona Clark, my consultant. She, like Mr Ayshford, was someone I immediately warmed to. She had an aura about her as she walked into the room. I stood as she introduced herself and shook my hand. She forewent the chair at the doctor's desk, choosing instead to jump up onto the bed positioned opposite the chair on which I was sitting. The way she spoke, even the way she sat on the bed, exuded confidence. Her obvious knowledge and expertise, combined with her delightful but at the same time no-nonsense manner, meant I instinctively trusted her and felt comfortable she was to oversee my chemotherapy.

She explained very clearly what the treatment procedure was and what would need to be done as part of that process. Whilst I listened intently, probably more intently than I have ever listened to anything in my life, I quickly became aware that much of what she was saying simply wasn't going in, such was the whirlwind of information, questions, concerns and anxieties slamming around inside my head.

Dr Clark discussed with me the chemotherapy I would be receiving. My ignorant, pre-cancer self had not appreciated there are different types of chemotherapy. I had always assumed it was a 'one-size-fits-all' situation. It transpired the typical chemotherapy for Hodgkin's lymphoma is ABVD, an acronym of the drugs used: Doxorubicin, originally called Adriamycin; Bleomycin; Vinblasine; Dacarbazine.

Although much of what we discussed and the information I was given became something of a blur, I do remember her telling me about the possible side effects of the treatment. Like most of us, I had a pre-conceived idea of what chemotherapy can do to a human being in addition to its primary task of killing cancerous cells in terms of hair loss, sickness etc. Whilst that stereotypical image unfortunately remains true for some, it was evident from what Dr Clark said that advances had been made in the drugs for treating side effects, and the different responses experienced by individual patients undergoing each type of chemotherapy, which meant it was impossible to predict what side effects I might encounter.

She also rather memorably confirmed Mr Ayshford's assessment that there was a thirty percent chance I would be dead within a year. I say memorably, because firstly that's not the sort of information one forgets in a hurry, and secondly there was an (albeit very small) unconscious part of me that had considered the possibility Mr Ayshford had got it wrong, and the likelihood of Patrick killing me was actually significantly less than the thirty percent he had reported. (He evidently hadn't made any such error.) Thirdly, because I distinctly remember thinking how blasé she appeared about it. I'm sure I was wrong in my assessment, but the rather matter-of-fact way she mentioned it gave me that impression.

Perhaps sensing my unease with the apparent ease with which she delivered such news, she quickly added, 'But you should not concern yourself unduly with that prospect, because we're going to treat the cancer in a very aggressive way.'

'Not concern yourself with that!?' Patrick piped up. 'Not concern yourself with the fact there's a thirty percent chance you'll be dead in a year. Wow! She's good. A little delusional perhaps, but good! I've not met her before, but I like her already.' He was sitting, arms folded, on the bed next to Dr Clark gazing up at her in almost respectful admiration. 'It takes a special kind of person to deliver such crushingly devastating news with so much confidence and apparent positivity,' he concluded with more than a degree of vitriol.

The rationale behind her assurance was that she

intended to 'blast' the cancer. I very much appreciated the sentiment of this instruction, and to not concern myself unduly, for an instruction it most certainly was. Dr Clark had already established herself as someone even a middle-aged, bloody-minded, stroppy bugger like me was not going to disobey. From that moment, and for the remainder of our relationship, if she told me to do something, I was going to do it.

Not being concerned about the thirty percent chance I could be substituted inside twelve months was rather easier said than done, but the willingness and very clear intention on Dr Clark's part to 'blast' my cancer and ensure I was cured (my word not hers) was incredibly reassuring. The flip side to this approach, as I was to very quickly discover, was that aggressive treatment has its consequences.

I RESEARCHED THE SHIT OUT OF IT

I immediately sought as much information as I could find about my specific cancer and the treatment I was going to have. One of my first sources of data was the booklets produced by MacMillan. I obtained several from the dedicated information centre at the hospital following my first meeting with Dr Clark.

Once back at home I made myself comfortable on my sofa and began delving into this plethora of information in an attempt to assimilate as much as possible and to garner a greater understanding of how matters progressed from here. Patrick sat next to me engrossed in his own reading material: *Ruining People's Lives for Dummies*.

The booklets were very readable and contained lots of useful information. However, such information is, by necessity, given the variances in cancer treatments and cancer patients' reactions to them, rather non-specific. As it transpired in my case rather misleadingly so.

Whilst the obtaining of relevant information is, of course, a good thing, and something I would encourage anyone who finds themselves in such a situation to do, it is also important to be aware of the pitfalls of becoming too readily assured that you have all the facts. Cancer is an almost uniquely personal and individual thing. Each of us will be treated differently and will respond in our own way to the treatment provided to us. Our bodies will absorb the toxins that are pumped into our systems in different ways, some far more easily than others, and our reactions to those drugs will vary considerably.

Visit any bookshop or library and you will find shelves full of books about cancer. Some are written by doctors, others by 'experts', and some, like this, by cancer patients/survivors. There are also those finished and/or published posthumously. Although all classified under the same subject heading, 'Cancer', they cover a vast range of approaches and information. Even a cursory scan of the titles will uncover information on what it's like to have and be treated for cancer written by those who know, standing cover to cover with books about what it's like to have cancer by those who actually have no idea – at least no practical, physical knowledge. Theoretical knowledge is a very different thing to real knowledge. A number of the titles I have seen and read make claims and offer advice that border on the absurd. Most disturbing are those books whose claims are fanciful in the extreme and cruelly misleading, offering, as they claim to do, advice on how to survive or prevent cancer.

My lack of understanding of cancer and my need to have a greater appreciation of the process I was about to embark on became an apparently insatiable thirst for knowledge. I would go as far as to say I became almost obsessed. I read copious books, articles and newspaper reports in my search for information regarding my condition, my treatment, and my future. In short, I researched the shit out of it.

The books I bought, along with those I borrowed from the library, filled a shelf in my bedroom ready to be read and their contents absorbed into my psyche. They were my accompaniment and time consumer at my early chemo sessions. It was a good way to pass the time while I was tethered to a machine dispensing poison into me, and the long hours spent alone at home when the children were with their mother or at school and I couldn't get my arse off the sofa. They were the saviour of my sanity when Patrick woke me in the middle of the night, determined to ensure the pains in my body over-ruled the fatigue that made sleep my primary objective. Reading something, anything, served as a distraction, although not always a very good one.

Reading the real-life stories of other cancer sufferers provided a degree of comfort and insight into this hideous world and the huge crock of shit into which I had been immersed. These incredibly touching stories certainly helped me to remain realistic about my own experiences and prevented me from becoming too consumed by self-pity.

Patrick was adept at manipulating the information I garnered from reading those stories in the mind games he loved to play. He was constantly trying to convert me to his perverse ways of thinking and to succumb to his philosophy, endlessly attempting to brainwash me with his evil propaganda and psychological machinations.

In one area, I am ashamed to admit, he succeeded in

converting me to the dark side, a force of enormous evil power, of which Patrick was the Imperial Overlord. I was powerless to resist his persuasions as he converted me to the sadistic facet of his nature. I took an altogether morbid, yet entirely unintentional, satisfaction from the suffering of others. The satisfaction came from the reassurance that I was not alone rather than from any gratification based on the misery and pain of my fellow sufferers, but it still made me feel incredibly uneasy.

The theory books I read were interesting for the general information they provided, particularly at the beginning of my journey into the unknown and the early stages of my treatment. They gave me at least some understanding of how my relationship with Patrick might pan out and what may lie ahead for us. However, by definition, such books can only provide a universal, non-specific insight into the world of cancer.

Patrick's world, the one I now inhabited, was one far removed from the non-cancer world I used to occupy. The uniqueness of my new situation, and of all those individuals who have put pen to paper, or fingers to keyboard, to record their experiences of cancer treatment, is borne out in those pages, and these. Many of these authors suffered far more than me, and for some their own very particular journey did not end well. Reading the stories of others going through their own experiences highlighted just how different each of our journeys are.

I'VE ALREADY GOT NO HAIR

No research into cancer would be complete without a significant rummage through the pages and chapters dedicated to the side effects of chemo. I was aware of my own preconceived ideas of how chemotherapy affects those undertaking it, had taken on board most of what Dr Clark told me about the possible side effects of my particular treatment, and set about conducting my own research, the idea being that the accumulation of this knowledge would prepare me for what lay ahead. It didn't.

'You can research all you want,' Patrick said, 'it won't make a blind bit of difference. It's all completely arbitrary, even I don't have complete control over it. It's a tombola of conditions. A lucky dip. You put your hand in and see what comes out. Some of the effects will be relatively minor, and you will hardly notice; others, the really good ones, will turn your life upside down. I can't wait to see what you're going to get.'

Despite the obvious excitement in my companion's voice and the degree of authority with which he spoke,

I ignored him and embarked on my research. I first consulted 'Understanding Chemotherapy', one of the range of booklets produced by Macmillan Cancer Support. This provided general information about chemotherapy – how chemotherapy drugs work, how chemotherapy is given, the possible physical side effects, and effects on everyday life etc.

More specifically informative was a Macmillan fact sheet, 'ABVD Chemotherapy'. Of particular interest to me was the list of side effects commonly experienced by patients having ABVD. The list was surprisingly and rather disturbingly lengthy and included: risk of infection, bruising or bleeding, anaemia, nausea, vomiting, fatigue, hair loss, sore mouth and ulcers, taste changes, heartburn and peripheral neuropathy (numbness and tingling in the hands or feet). There was more: extravasation (damage caused by leakage of the drugs into the tissue around the vein causing damage to the area), allergic reaction, fevers and chills, skin changes, changes in nails, changes in the way your heart works and changes to the lungs.

Last in the list was changes to sex life. This final item seemed something of an unnecessary inclusion, given the conditions listed above it. It was difficult to imagine a situation where, whilst experiencing even some of the conditions on the list, I would even want to have sex. Even more relevant was the fact that, even if I had wanted to, any sex to be had would be subject to finding someone who would want to share the experience with me. This also seemed increasingly unlikely in light of the list of the very sexy and utterly endearing side effects that could be heading my way. I couldn't help thinking this cancer lark was clearly going to be an absolute blast. But as I read the list, I tried to console myself that these were only *possible* side effects. I might be lucky.

'We'll see,' Patrick chuckled, in the way of someone who knows for certain that your understanding of something is incorrect whilst theirs is spot on, but they're happy to go on letting you believe you may be right.

I also started to imagine what it might be like to have any of these side effects inflicted on me and how I would cope with each of them. Admittedly some of the more obviously worrying ones – changes to heart and lungs, and extravasation – were a little concerning, but I thought I could cope with most of the others.

Tiredness. Everyone knows how it feels to be tired. I could hear Patrick's mischievous little voice in my head again: 'You've had three kids, Fry, you know tired.'

He wasn't wrong. I hadn't slept properly for six years after Mollie was born, as she and the siblings who followed her all settled into nightly routines of not sleeping. I could do that again. If I wasn't going to be at work, I would just sleep when the children were at school. Wrong.

Nausea and vomiting. Easy. It'll be like having a hangover. Nothing a bacon roll wouldn't solve. Wrong.

We've all had ulcers and a fever, and how difficult can a bit of numbness be to deal with?

'I think you might be missing the point here, Fry,' Patrick interjected.

I continued to scour the list, while Patrick sat on the back of the sofa behind me, peering over my shoulder.

Of all the possible side effects listed, I was instinctively drawn to one – the possibility of hair loss. I already had no hair. Imagine Jason Statham, Bruce Willis or the Mitchell Brothers and you'll have an idea of the follicularly challenged nature of my head covering. Hair loss I could most definitely deal with. I completely understand how devastating hair loss can be for those, mostly women, for whom their hair is an intrinsic part of their identity, but losing what little hair I had left would make bugger all difference to me. It would simply mean I didn't have to shave my head as regularly as I currently did. Yes, a plus to chemotherapy!

'So you'd be happy with that one, would you?' said Patrick inquisitively. 'You know that some cancer sufferers who lose their hair find that their post-chemo hair is very different to what they had prior to their treatment? Sometimes curlier, sometimes straighter, and now and then a completely different colour.'

I had read about this possibility, but somehow having Patrick's confirmation made the chances all the more real. I would be lying if I didn't, albeit briefly, consider what it would be like to have hair again. I even contemplated what I would look like with a ginger afro.

It never happened, neither the hair loss nor the ginger afro. In what was unquestionably the most ironic moment of the whole of our time together, and one which Patrick must have had some input into, hair loss would be the one side effect I wouldn't get, at least not on my head. My facial hair didn't grow for six months, and I still have two bare patches on the backs of my legs. This was most definitely Patrick's idea of having a laugh with me. I can still hear him giggling in my ear, 'Giving you hair loss would have been far too easy.'

With a further delve into his lucky dip of side

effects, Patrick provided an additional little surprise for me. Shortly after I began my treatment, I noticed a drooping of my left eye. I sought the advice of Dr Clark, who diagnosed Horner's syndrome. Just one of the additional delights Patrick presented me with.

'That one's not even on the list!' Patrick laughed, taunting me. 'Think of it as a special Patrick bonus,' he added with irrepressible delight.

BEFORE WE BEGIN

Before my chemotherapy could begin, Patrick had organised several tests and appointments for me. As well as his self-appointed position as the wannabe destroyer of my life, he had also made himself my personal assistant. He took this role rather too seriously and began arranging and organising every facet of my life without consulting me about anything.

Additionally, he took it upon himself to become my chaperone, accompanying me to all my appointments, never letting me out of his sight. However, perhaps not surprisingly, he lacked some of the fundamental skills required for this rather sensitive position. He had clearly been absent from chaperone school on the day they covered the primary functions of such a person, i.e. to look after and provide emotional support to their charge. He was shit. Instead of looking after and supporting me he was nothing more than a sadistic voyeur revelling in the pain and suffering he was causing me. He loved it. He couldn't get enough of it.

First on the itinerary compiled by my overzealous

PA was the taking of a sample of bone marrow. This procedure, performed under local anaesthetic, is common in cancers such as mine, but also leukaemia and myeloma. It involves the insertion of a syringe into the hip bone and the removal of bone marrow cells which can then be examined to establish whether or not they contain any cancerous cells.

Dr Clark performed the procedure. Patrick sat on the counter at the edge of the room, his little legs hanging over the side, observing proceedings as Dr Clark produced from a drawer immediately adjacent to where my little companion sat a syringe so big one could have been forgiven for thinking it was actually a piece of zoological equipment a vet might use to vaccinate an elephant.

On seeing this hideous-looking piece of modern-day torturing apparatus Patrick leapt to his feet, jumped up and down on the counter and began clapping his hands together, hardly able to contain his unbridled joy.

'Look at the size of that,' he said with a degree of awe and wonder. 'That is enormous. This is going to be fun,' he laughed.

I was already becoming strangely tolerant and accepting of Patrick, his ways and the crusade he was on to take over my life. Obviously, I hated the little fucker, but I was getting used to him. So, it wasn't too difficult to ignore his joyful commentary as Dr Clark began the procedure.

It was certainly not the most comfortable thing I have ever experienced. Such was the length of the needle that as it was plunged deeper and deeper into my body it felt as though she was drilling into my hip. I was half expecting the thing to go right through me, skewering me to the bed like a human kebab. This assessment was in fact somewhat closer to the reality of the situation than I was really prepared to accept. The amount of force Dr Clark was having to use was more than a little disconcerting. Although I was lying turned away from her, I could just about see what she was doing out of the corner of my eye, and I swear at one point she had both feet off the floor and was actually kneeling on the edge of the bed using all her body weight to force this piece of medical paraphernalia into me.

'This is great!' Patrick exclaimed, still clapping his hands, almost giddy with excitement. 'I love it! I love it!'

This most bizarre of experiences was over relatively quickly and the aching in the bone passed in no time. Although having Dr Clark drill into me had meant another visit to the hospital, it was at least, I thought, one of Patrick's 'things to do' we could tick off the list. Little did I know that as the months went by the list of tests, scans, procedures and treatments would grow as rapidly as an NHS waiting list, and I would very soon become so hacked off with it all that 'ticking off' became a completely futile and meaningless exercise and provided not even the slightest sense of relief.

'One down, lots, lots more to go,' Patrick declared as we left the hospital. 'What's next?' he asked rhetorically. He thought for a moment. 'Oh yes, I know.' He smiled.

Next on the list of the whirlwind of appointments, scans and procedures was my standard 'pre-chemo appointment'. This was a longer meeting with both Dr Clark and my key worker, Peter James. Both spent a considerable amount of time taking me through, in more detail, my treatment, the procedures and possible side effects. The discussions were handled very sensitively, and I was given every opportunity to ask questions about my chemotherapy. Despite this, throughout both meetings, and as the load of information I was carrying began to crush me, my overriding feeling was one of how surreal it all felt. Was this really happening to me? Was this really to be my life for the next seven months? Was I really being followed around by a talking teddy bear who was trying to kill me?

Being told by Dr Clark that there are no-nos when it came to what I could and couldn't do when having chemotherapy, confirmed for me that I would simply go on living my life as normal. I would go to work, look after my children and coach my football team.

'We'll see about that,' said Patrick. 'You seem to be forgetting something.' He smashed his hands together as if playing the cymbals. 'You've forgotten about the trucks.'

I had to think for a moment to make sense of this rather oblique reference. I got there eventually. He was referring to the fact I had chosen to overlook that Dr Clark had also said there may be days when I would feel like I'd been 'hit by a truck' and wouldn't be able to do anything. Although, at the time, I may have allowed that particular piece of information to slip almost unnoticed into my subconscious, it clearly made an impression because it was one I used many times thereafter to describe how I felt.

During our chat Peter gave me a small blue ring binder folder. This contained various pieces of information and forms which were to be completed and signed by the medical professionals looking after me. It felt rather like the sort of report card that an unruly child might be given at school and is required to take to each lesson for their teachers to sign to confirm they had both attended and behaved in the requisite way. This folder was to accompany me and Patrick to every appointment from that moment forward to confirm both my attendance and good behaviour.

Whilst I very much appreciated the very real and genuine care I was being given, I found it impossible to think coherently, organise my thoughts, articulate my feelings and raise any questions I had. Everything was such a blur.

Patrick had been conspicuous by his absence throughout most of my discussions with Peter and Dr Clark, and when he reappeared he was unusually silent. There were no barbed comments or sensational commentary. His lack of meddling was both puzzling and unnerving in equal measure. But then he became visibly more and more agitated, until it all got too much for him. He jumped down from the chair on which he had perched himself and with a tone of indignation barked, 'This is boring. No pain or discomfort, no intrusive procedures. Boring! In fact, I've had enough. I'm off. I'll wait for you outside.' With that he stormed out of the room, slamming the door behind him.

Although the day had been pain- discomfort- and procedure-free, Patrick may have been a little premature in his decision to depart the scene.

One thing I did ask Peter was if I could see the room where I would have my chemo. In an attempt to lighten the situation a little I explained I had this vision in my head of a space akin to the lounge in an old people's home, with lots of high-backed chairs positioned around the outside of the room.

He paused briefly, then laughed. 'It's just like that,' he chuckled, 'just without a telly.'

I had assumed he was joking. But as I stepped tentatively into the room, immediately adjacent to the consulting room where I had first met Dr Clark, I realised he wasn't. My heart sank. There were indeed a large number of high-backed chairs, all tightly grouped around the edges of the room. So close together were they that they afforded almost no privacy to their occupants. Scattered around the room were a number of patients, all considerably older than me, all of whom looked extremely ill. The vision before me was a room with very few endearing features.

The floor had apparently been mopped and bleached within an inch of its life and was so clean it was almost reflective.

The chairs were not at all aesthetically pleasing. The other little bits of furniture, side tables etc., looked like they had been acquired from an end-of-stock sale sometime in the '80s. It looked like a furniture elephants' graveyard; a place where old, discarded furniture goes to die.

In a rather desperate and somewhat forlorn attempt to take something positive from this whole experience I noted that, on one side, the entire wall was taken up with a window which afforded a huge amount of light to flood into the space. The sunlight combined with the white walls and floor made the room incredibly bright and warming. It was almost as if the decision had been taken to make the room as bright as possible, thus providing surroundings in direct contrast to the darkness of the feelings of those who inhabited it. Casting such a huge amount of light into the room did add to its clinical appearance, however, but I christened it the 'Sunshine Room'. Although such a name sounds more akin to that of a playroom at a kindergarten rather than the place where a random, diverse collection of people come to be poisoned, it seemed a most apt description.

As I scanned the room my eye was drawn to a familiar sight in the far corner.

'This is nice,' Patrick commented, and joined us as we wandered around, like an estate agent valuing a new property, assessing every little facet of the room. 'Not too bad at all,' was his considered professional opinion. He continued his judgement as he jumped up onto one of the vacant chairs and proceeded to bounce up and down. 'Comfy. Pleasant, bright room. Nice neighbours, and they provide tea. All in all, not too shabby. We'll be fine here, Fry.' Not for the first time, our assessments differed somewhat.

I could not imagine spending any time in this room, let alone being imprisoned here for a day every two weeks for the next six months. I felt sicker and more utterly deflated than I had at the beginning of the day. I was tempted to tell Peter I wasn't going to do it: Thank you for all your help and advice, but I've decided I'm going to leave it, if that's okay. I won't be coming in tomorrow; I'll take my chances without the treatment.

Even though Patrick had by now disappeared again – he was probably off causing mischief at the nurses' station or wrecking a stock cupboard somewhere – I was fully aware what his reaction would have been: You have to come back tomorrow. If you don't have the treatment you won't suffer nearly as much. Why would you ruin my fun? Why?

He would have loved this internal dilemma. Do I refuse treatment and allow Patrick to slowly consume more of my body and face the certainty of him eventually killing me, or do I suck it up, zip up my man suit, do the sensible thing and get on with the treatment and take whatever was to come my way? There was only one option.

'See you tomorrow, Peter,' I said, shook his hand and left.

As I made my way out of the Rowan Suite I was unsure as to which part of my Sunshine Room initiation was more dispiriting; the prospect of undertaking six months of treatment in that room, or the realisation that Patrick had already become such an intrinsic part of my life I could see him everywhere I went and was able to accurately second guess how he would react in any given situation.

Patrick and I were reunited outside the hospital ready for our walk home. He was holding two chocolate bars in his paw. He held them out towards me.

'Do you want one? I got them from the hospital shop. I do love a hospital shop. One's for you.'

I simply shook my head in disbelief. Disbelief we had got to a stage where I was now being offered chocolate by a teddy bear that existed only in my head. Even more extraordinary was that I turned down a bar of chocolate. I didn't even want to think about where he got the money to pay for them.

'I'm glad I came back. That's a nice room. I liked it.'

A smile spread slowly across his little furry face. The

rest of our walk home took place in silence, primarily because Patrick spent the whole journey stuffing his face with BOTH chocolate bars.

Having already had MRI and CT scans, I was sent for a PET CT scan. A PET CT scan, not unsurprisingly given its name, combines a CT scan and a PET scan. One of the doctors explained the difference by describing a CT scan as a black and white image, while a PET CT produces a picture in glorious technicolour. The scan takes a series of x-rays from all around your body and puts them together to create a three-dimensional picture.

For this appointment Patrick and I drove to a private clinic approximately forty miles from home. The clinic was, as you might expect, somewhat different to the NHS hospitals and facilities I'd had the pleasure of attending. It was beautifully decorated, calming, comfortable, with tea and coffee on tap. It was most definitely not the most unpleasant environment Patrick and I had visited.

'I don't like this,' Patrick declared as we sat in the very comfortable waiting area. 'This is much too nice. Far too comfortable. The sooner I can get you out of here and back to normality the better.' He plonked himself down in one of the comfy chairs, crossed his arms and sulked.

Before the scan, I was injected with a radioactive solution that would circulate around my body highlighting cells that are more active than normal, i.e. cancerous cells. I was then made to rest for approximately an hour while the solution did its work. Naturally, I protested vigorously about the idea of lying on a very comfortable bed listening to soothing music, but they were insistent. So, in the interests of compliance, I reluctantly agreed.

'You comfortable?' Patrick asked. He seemed agitated.

I really am, I thought as I lay on the bed, eyes closed, the sound of the music wafting around me. This was the first time in a while I had felt genuinely relaxed, and I was determined to make the most of it.

'Oh, for fuck's sake!' Patrick snapped, and with that he again retreated to wait for me in the comfort and less frustrating environment of the car.

Scan taken and another test/appointment dutifully completed, I drove home to prepare myself for whatever Patrick was to throw at me next. I didn't have to wait very long.

MY MASTURBATION PRISON CELL

The subject of infertility as a result of chemotherapy was another issue raised before I began my treatment. I was asked to consider the option of having my sperm frozen in the event my treatment had a dramatically negative impact on my swimmers. I already had three beautiful children but, given that I was single, and one never knows what might happen in the future, I decided I would keep a little supply, just in case.

This decision necessitated a trip to yet another hospital, thirty miles from home, to provide my sample – a more stressful exercise than one might imagine.

Once at the hospital, and having made my way to the appropriate unit, I was greeted by a male nurse. He took me to a consulting room where he explained, at some length, the procedure regarding the freezing of my sperm, the legal details surrounding how it would be stored and my rights to access, use, destruction etc. He then gave me the cup into which I was to 'deposit my sample' and asked me to follow him to the room in which I was to produce the said sample.

As we made our way along the corridor we were joined by Patrick. He had been with me when we arrived at the hospital but had wandered off almost as soon as we had walked through the main entrance.

What happened next is unquestionably one of the strangest things that has ever happened to me. I spoke to him. I spoke to this abomination I had created and which was merely an occupant of my mind. Patrick and I had our first proper conversation.

The most extraordinary thing about this decision to engage with my cuddly companion was that it felt entirely ordinary. Up to this point our conversations had been an internal silent dialogue confined to the inner sanctum of my head. I had become accustomed to his constant presence, his input, his observations and disparaging comments. He was now such a fundamental part of this new stage of my life that I felt able to do more than just listen to and absorb his oral contributions and embarked on a dialogue with him for the first time.

I fell several paces behind my nurse escort so I could talk to Patrick without being heard. I may have been ready to speak to my imaginary companion, but I felt the rest of the world was not yet ready for such a development and might find the whole business a little difficult to comprehend.

'Where have you been?' I whispered rather nervously, genuinely curious as to what could possibly have distracted him from what I had imagined would be his uncontrollable need to gloat about the successful implementation of the latest instalment in the 'let's make life as uncomfortable for Fry as we possibly can' project.

'Why? Did you miss me?' he smirked. This was a facial expression I was to see far too frequently during the following months. It always engendered in me the same violent reaction. It made me want to punch him on his smug furry little nose.

He didn't wait for an answer before explaining his absence. 'I went to get these.' He held up a chocolate bar in one paw and a book of raffle tickets in the other.

'You do know it is not mandatory to visit the shop every time we are at a hospital?' I asked, knowing all too well how much Patrick loved the hospital shop and that for him, just as for any child visiting the hospital, a visit to the hospital shop to buy sweets you don't need is indeed mandatory. 'What are they for?'

'I was hungry.'

'Not the chocolate! Those!' I pointed to the book of tickets he was clutching.

'Oh. I had an idea. I thought I could sell tickets for your little show.'

'What show?' I asked, genuinely not understanding what he meant.

'Your 'sample' show.'

I remained utterly confused about what on earth he was talking about. I was beginning to regret the whole 'let's have a chat' decision…and then the reality of what he was suggesting suddenly dawned on me.

'What!? Are you completely mad!? It's not some kind of spectator sport! So, it's not enough for you to have put me in this position in the first place, creating a situation where I have to do a sixty-mile round trip to wank into a cup. Now you want to make some money at my expense too!' I paused momentarily to fully digest Patrick's suggestion, before adding, 'You seem to be overlooking one tiny little factor, my fiscally challenged friend. No one, but no one, is going to want to pay money to watch me do what I am about to do.'

My furry companion looked more than a little confused.

'You mean you're not here to do some kind of set?'

'What? A set?' Patrick wasn't alone in his confusion.

'Yes, a set. When you mentioned producing a sample, I thought we were here for you to do some kind of music demo you'd put together. Is that not right?'

'No, that's not right. Think about where we are, you stupid little moron. What kind of sample do you think I might be here to produce?'

As the penny dropped Patrick's expression changed from one of confusion to utter dejection, his money-making scheme lying in tatters around his feet. He was utterly forlorn, like an entrepreneur who has just had his genius idea dismissed out of hand by a resounding chorus of 'I'm out' from the assembled Dragons, and was leaving the den without any form of support, financial or otherwise, his dreams of fame and wealth crushed beyond recognition with the uttering of those two little words. If only it had been that easy for me to rid myself of Patrick and send him away with a flea in his ear.

The nurse glanced over his shoulder and interrupted. I was rather relieved he had disturbed this most bizarre of conversations. 'The room is on a busy corridor so don't be put off if you hear chatting or laughing while you're in there,' he explained.

I had apparently inadvertently become an extra in a Carry-On film. I didn't remember signing up for that. I was now imagining groups of young nurses walking along the corridor giggling as they passed the room in which they know a man is producing a 'sample'. Given my newly acquired place in this innuendo-filled farce, I half expected to get to the room and find a sign on the door informing passers-by, 'Wanking in progress. Do not disturb'. There was no such sign, but there might as well have been given how self-conscious I was feeling as he showed me into the room.

'Press this bell when you're finished, and I will come back to collect you,' he said, pointing to a doorbell on the wall just inside the door.

With that he shut the door and left, locking it from the outside, leaving me alone in the room with just my cup and an increasing feeling of self-consciousness. As the door closed, I could hear Patrick behind me, mumbling about lost financial opportunities and how he was going to prove me wrong. I spun around.

'What the fuck are you doing in here? Oh great. So, I'm here, locked in a room, on a busy corridor, apparently the source of much hysteria on the part of all and sundry who may just wander past, with a cup in my hand, while a nurse waits for me to press a bell to inform him I've *finished*. Now, just when things couldn't get any weirder, you're here too! I am already maxed out in the uncomfortable stakes; I certainly don't need a bloody audience as well. Perhaps I should just go and do it in the middle of the corridor and eliminate all the pretence!? Get out!'

Just minutes after the start of our first conversation we were now having our first argument.

'Alright, calm down. I can't leave now. He's locked the door,' Patrick replied, correctly identifying the significant obstacle to him complying with my request.

'I didn't intend to join you, I just followed you in here. I follow you everywhere now. Wherever you go, I go. It's become a reflex.'

'So you are literally never going to leave me alone?' I asked, trying to seek some clarification of the terms and conditions of this new arrangement I had unwittingly become involved in.

'Nope,' came the very smug, self-satisfied, barely audible reply through a mouthful of semi-chewed chocolate. 'It's alright, I won't look.' He turned his back and covered his eyes with the book of now redundant tickets and continued mumbling about his lost revenue and how we had both missed out on the opportunity to make a few quid.

'By the way. Did you get me one of those?' I asked in an attempt to lighten the atmosphere a little, pointing at the half-eaten chocolate bar.

Patrick gradually lowered the tickets from his eyes, turned his head, looked me straight in the eye and grinned. 'Nope!'

The room I was imprisoned in was pleasant enough – sofa, coffee table, basin, nice but nondescript pictures on the neutral-coloured walls. On the table was a red ring binder folder labelled 'Adult Literature'. Just for a moment I thought how nice it was of the hospital to provide its customers with something to read. I opened it naively, anticipating reading material for the more discerning mature reader, perhaps a Henry James, Balzac, Proust, Tolstoy or some other literary classics. 'Bloody hell, how long do they expect me to be in here? I'm not sure I'll have time to read *War and Peace*.'

It wasn't that kind of adult literature. I found within the covers of the binder exactly what one would expect to find in a folder in such a room and given the reason I was there. Describing the contents as 'literature' may have been overstating matters somewhat. I can't imagine many of those pages had ever been read.

Each page of the folder's contents was laminated, and hole punched, but very few were actually held within its rings; most simply lay loose.

I could hear Patrick posing questions that started to vex me: 'How long do you think you're expected to be? I wonder what the average time to produce a 'sample' is? I bet they keep unofficial stats for that kind of thing and you'll be ranked accordingly.'

'No. Do you think? Surely not.' I was now in such a state of paranoia I would have believed pretty much anything anyone would have told me about this most bizarre of situations I'd found myself in.

There was a brief pause as Patrick swallowed a mouthful of chocolate. 'I wouldn't worry too much if I were you. I don't think there's any danger of you coming out of this very well. I bet you'll be distinctly second division!' He paused as he glanced around the room. 'Do you think there are hidden cameras?'

'What!? No!' I replied instinctively before having a cursory look for evidence of any spying eyes. 'Shut up and eat your chocolate.'

Self-consciousness, speed and judging criteria put sufficiently to one side and sample duly deposited, I rang the bell to indicate that I had 'finished'. While I waited, cup in hand, for the nurse to return, the OCD part of me kicked in and I was overcome by a need to reattach all the pages of the adult material neatly back, in order, to the rings in the folder. I did so and placed it on the table ready for the next occupant. The nurse opened the door to release me from my masturbation prison cell and took the container from me.

On the way back to the office, he showed me the room in which my cup full of (I say full; containing would be more accurate) sperm was to be frozen and stored. A brief conversation took place in the office. I shook the nurse's hand (I had washed it – mine not his) and thanked him for his time and advice. 'Thank you for coming,' he said, with not even the slightest amount of irony or intention to be funny. Patrick sniggered. I said nothing and left.

Copies of the legal paperwork in hand, I left my swimmers in the care of the staff and made my way out of the hospital. On the way I passed the nurses' station, where a trio of female staff stood chatting. My levels of self-consciousness soared again, to such an extent I almost lost the ability to walk. Ordinarily I would have said something as I passed, bidding them all a good day or some such pleasantry. Not today. I hurried passed in silence, head down as I imagined them, hands over their mouths, attempting to suppress their giggles, discussing me as I left. 'He was the quickest this week' or 'He was obviously having far too much fun; he was in there forever!'

I drove home having completed yet another, if one of the rather more surreal, of the appointments Patrick had arranged for me. He was clearly very satisfied with his day's work, but something was still bothering him. From the moment we left the hospital he was agitated and restless. He sat in the passenger seat next to me, clutching his now redundant purchase, and asked, rather pointedly, 'What the hell am I going to do with these bloody tickets?'

WHO AM I NOW?

Identity is just one part of everyday life that very quickly disappears when you are receiving treatment for cancer. Patrick's intervention ensured that others immediately saw me only in that context; no longer as a person, an individual, but as someone who has cancer. I became a walking (often with difficulty) medical condition. I ceased to be the person I was – father, professional, friend, football coach – and was replaced by a person unrecognisable, sometimes literally, from the one I was before I was told I had cancer and Patrick became a permanent appendage to my life. I was unable to be the father I was prior to my cancer day. My other primary identity, Mr Fry, teacher man, ceased to exist completely.

I wanted so much to retain those personas, any of those personas. I was desperate to preserve some semblance of the pre-Patrick me. I resisted, as much as I could, Patrick's determination to strip me of my personality, but he wanted me to be seen only in the context of our relationship. I was desperate for someone to still see me as a father, teacher, football coach and not merely as Ian Fry, cancer sufferer. I was, still am and remained throughout my treatment to a greater or lesser extent, Daddy – to my children, Mr Fry – to my pupils, Gaffer – to my football team. I was all of these people before I got cancer and I would be all those people once Patrick had buggered off.

Although I have now given up my role as football coach, I am still Daddy and Mr Fry. I also have a past, a life before I became Ian Fry, cancer sufferer, which has its own relevance on my journey. A life that Patrick was so eager to destroy.

The day after I was told I had cancer I saw a TV advert for MacMillan cancer care. It was an advert I had seen before but one which until now I had not connected with or paid any particular notice to. The advert emphasised the work MacMillan does in support of those living with cancer. The strap line at the end stated, 'No one should face cancer alone'. As I sat, alone, watching that advert it suddenly dawned on me that living with cancer alone was exactly what I was about to do.

As a forty-three-year-old primary school teacher, twice divorced, and now single father of three – Mollie who was seven, Libby who was five, and Will who was four – custody of whom I share with their mother, my life was spectacular only in its conformity and apparent mundanity. Despite the lack of originality, it was a life, I thought, that had some meaning and purpose as father, teacher and coach. These were the roles that defined me, and I was proud of being all of these people. All in all, it was not the sort of life anyone would want to make a film about. It certainly would not feature in a collection of 'History's Most Exciting Lives', but it was one I enjoyed.

I was born in East London in January 1970. My parents divorced when I was seven, leaving me and my sister Amanda, who is sixteen months my junior, with our mum. We later lived with my mother's second husband and my half-brother Martin (thirteen years younger than me), and later still with her third husband.

I grew up in Redbridge in Northeast London, attending the local primary school and then the comprehensive one hundred yards from our house. I always hated school, which is ironic given what I ended up doing for a living, and consequently underachieved significantly. I left school with O Levels and A Levels, but in both cases neither the number nor grades I should have got.

I left home when I was eighteen and rented a room in a house in South Woodford, East London. I got a job at a bank in the City. A bank where my father was one of the personnel managers. Although that obviously had nothing to do with me getting the job. Nepotism is a wonderful thing! It turned out it was not a job for me. I detested everything about it and left after just three months.

I joined the civil service and met my first wife Sally, a barrister. I moved to Barnes in West London. We got married in June 1994 and divorced in 1997. During that time, I took a job at the Old Bailey. In my many years there, I performed a number of roles, but was primarily a court clerk. I loved working there. There is something very special about working in such a famous building; a building with such a history, but one which is also at the forefront of modern life. Working on such high-profile criminal cases gave me a real sense of excitement and an attachment to the tradition and history of our judicial system.

It was whilst working as a court clerk that I was, for a very short time, the centre of a national news story. In January 2001, the judge with whom I was sitting, HHJ Ann Goddard QC, was attacked by the defendant in the case she was hearing. He escaped from the dock, threw a carafe of water at her and rained a series of punches down on this defenceless sixty-four-year-old woman. I grabbed her assailant, pulled him away and wrestled him to the ground. We were joined in our little tussle by a police officer, who took over and dealt with the defendant while I escorted the judge back to her chambers and summoned medical help for her. The coverage the attack received on the national television news that evening and in the following day's newspapers ensured it was a big story for all of twenty-four hours. The incident itself was over in a matter of seconds, but for me that was my fifteen minutes.

I moved back to East London whilst at the Old Bailey and met my second wife Melanie, also a barrister, in 2002. We were married in 2003, the same year I gave up my job at the Old Bailey to pursue my long-wished-for dream of becoming a primary school teacher.

Melanie and I had our two beautiful girls, Mollie and Elizabeth, in London before moving to Worcester in April 2008 in order for me to take up a new teaching job. We divorced in 2012, but not before having our wonderful son William.

One of my primary concerns when I was told I had cancer, and one of the first things I queried with my consultant, was how I was going to be able to continue to work. I loved every aspect of my job, and it was, other than being a father, my most important role. Being a teacher defined me as a person. That was who I was. Not being at work would be one of the hardest things to deal with during those many months and would remove one of those fundamental elements that made me who I was.

I also continued to coach Droitwich Spa Ladies FC, a club I had been instrumental in forming just two years earlier. I was diagnosed during the closed season. The first three months of the following season coincided with the second half of my treatment. As the chemotherapy took a greater toll on my body during those last three months, performing my coaching role became increasingly difficult. On several occasions I was too weak to attend training sessions, and more than once had to leave the girls during their warm-up or the dugout during matches to take myself off to throw up behind a tree somewhere.

'Why don't you just give it up, Fry?' Patrick would often ask. It was clear he wanted me to pack it in.

But such a submission to Patrick's will would constitute another success for him in his quest to ruin my life and destroy me as a person.

'I don't want to. I love managing this team,' was the honest answer. 'Plus, if I do give up then that will be another victory for you, and I'm not having that.'

Although continuing in that role was far from easy, managing and coaching that team took on an importance all of its own during my treatment and beyond.

FUTURE – WHAT FUTURE?

Before Patrick came crashing into my life, any particular thoughts I did give to what life might have in store for me was fairly limited in its scope. My future, at least my conscious, considered future, largely revolved around my children. My short-term future included Will starting school in September, and Mollie and Libby moving into the junior school and year 1 respectively. Longer term I also had all the plans, aspirations and hopes all parents have for their children.

My own future was about educating and developing the children whose care I was entrusted with at work. My future was also my role as coach of Droitwich Spa Ladies FC and making them into the strongest and most successful team as I could. My future included the possibility of finding someone foolish and misguided enough to want to spend time with me.

As futures go it certainly wasn't very rock 'n' roll, not your all-action 'see the world, get promoted, buy your dream home, do all the things one should do before you're dead', but I was happy with it. It was good enough for me. Not hugely exciting, but good enough.

Suddenly, my future became rather more stark, more immediate, far more short term, and definitely more self-focussed. With the diagnosis and that shortest but most significant of sentences, 'You have cancer', my future became a series of very short-term questions. Will my body work tomorrow? When is my next chemo session? Will I be able to get out of bed? When is my next chemo session? How long will I feel utterly shit for this week? When is my next chemo session? Will I be able/want to eat today? When is my next chemo session? Will I be dead by this time next year? When is my next chemo session?

My future changed from being non time specific and apparently without end to something much simpler. My future was now limited to the next six months. It stopped on November 20th, the day of my last treatment. Thinking even a day past that date was pointless. Come November 20th, one of three new possible futures would present themselves.

I would be given the 'all clear': Patrick's gone, now get on with your life, Fry. Then I could have a future of my own again, based on my children and the fairly average things I wanted to do, see or experience.

Or I might be told that Patrick had decided to stick around for a bit longer. We hadn't been sufficiently vile to him to make him want to leave. Instead, he had decided to stay to continue his attempt to take over my body and make my future a Groundhog Day of chemotherapy-induced shit.

The third alternative would be that November 20th became the beginning of the end. I would be told that

Patrick, like a group of travellers commandeering and setting up home in a local field, had hijacked my body, decided he liked it so much that he had established a permanent place of residence, soon extending into neighbouring organs with a stated and very clear intention of taking everything he can, making the life of all the other organs thoroughly miserable until the local community [me] dies. As futures go, not great. Hardly in fact a future at all, very much a present.

One of these possibilities would become my 'new' future. First, however, I had to fulfil my current future, the one that ended on November 20th.

Whilst contemplating these futures it occurred to me just how much we all take our long-term future for granted. How often we very glibly think about the destination for next year's holiday, important landmarks in our children's future often years away, wedding dates years after getting engaged, the football World Cup or Olympics in four years' time, the outcome of the next General Election, without giving even a second thought to the fact we may not actually be here. We all make plans and assessments assuming we will be around to experience all those things. However glib such an approach may be, that is as it should be, particularly at the relatively young age of forty-three. We cannot and should not live our lives in fear they may be cut short and we may not see out at least our three score years and ten.

As I contemplated all I had been told since my diagnosis and what was in store for me, I began to reassess my future. I still had one, but mine was now almost exclusively about me and Patrick and only now lasted with any certainty until November.

It is good and healthy to make plans for a future. However, when faced with the very real – in my case, thirty percent – possibility I would be dead in a year it does alter one's perspective and attitude about making those kinds of plans, given they are ultimately based on an assumption, i.e. an assumption that any of us will still be alive in a year. Of course, I had to, and I did, assume I would be one of the seventy percent of people who survive my particular brand of 'good' cancer for twelve months or more, but planning beyond the end of November seemed rather pointless and something of a waste of time. I definitely wasn't going to be buying tickets for the Lord's test next summer, planning a fantastic holiday or scheduling a trip to watch England in the next World Cup. Making that particular plan certainly was a waste of time, but not because of the cancer. At the time England hadn't even qualified, and it's England!

YOU'RE SUCH AN IDIOT, FRY

Patrick and I had arrived at the evening before my first outing to the Sunshine Room and the start of my chemotherapy. Our fledgling relationship had reached its eighteenth day. Despite having known Patrick for less than three weeks, he had already established himself as fundamental a part of my life as my children, my job, West Ham United, the England cricket team, tea and chocolate digestives.

The previous twelve days had been such a whirlwind of appointments, a barrage of information, tests and scans. I hadn't really had time to properly take it all in.

As I went to bed that night, I started to feel rather differently about the next part of the journey Patrick had planned for me. I lay there trying to order my thoughts about my adventure with Patrick and exactly what it all meant for me. There was a remarkable and disturbing change in my thought processes. It was as if Patrick had turned off the switch marked 'surreal' and switched on the 'all too real' one next to it.

All the information I had been given and collected suddenly began to sink in and I now realised that the invincibility cloak, which I had worn for so long and convinced myself was impenetrable, was actually riddled with holes. The enormity of what I was about to do and just how hideous this whole process might be started to dawn on me.

I felt rather ashamed and embarrassed that I had been so spectacularly stupid. How could it be that I had been so reluctant to face reality? Why had I not been more willing to take on board everything I had read and been told? This fantastically naïve and ignorant approach had resulted in me being just hours away from the start of my chemotherapy and finding myself utterly unprepared for what lay in wait.

I was reminded of all those days when I was at school and I would leave my homework until the last possible moment. It didn't matter what subject it was, the time I had been given to complete it or how much had to be done, it would always get completed the night before it was due in, after I'd done all the far more important things I had to do – playing football or cricket or watching what I wanted on the television, and that was in the '80s when the choice of viewing pleasure available to us was minuscule compared to the distractions kids have today. We didn't have Netflix, YouTube, the internet or Instagram. Christ, if I was at school now, I'd never get any homework done!

I vividly recall one particular evening when I was studying for my A Levels. I say studying…being a lazy toad, doing as little work as possible and hoping for the best, would be a more accurate description. I had two essays to be handed in on the same day. I left both until the evening before the submission date and had to work through the night to get them completed for fear of what a failure to hand them in on time would bring.

I was always a bit of a rebel at school, albeit one with a firm grasp on what was right and wrong, with very clearly defined lines that I would not cross. James Dean I was most definitely not.

I did get my ears pierced when I was thirteen, much to the headmaster's chagrin. When he called me into his office to take me to task about it, he was so angry I actually thought he was going to explode. The situation wasn't helped by me pointing out to him that 'The girls are allowed to wear earrings, so why can't I?' In addition to this very 1980's fashion statement, I frequently and blatantly flouted the school's uniform policy. I would wear distinctly non-uniform jumpers and white socks. In the '80s wearing white socks to school was the most heinous of social contraventions, at least it was at my East London comprehensive. I never really understood why the wearing of 'inappropriate' socks was such an issue. When one thinks about clothing that makes a statement, a declaration of defiance, one thinks of leather jackets, Dr Marten boots, short skirts. Socks do not immediately leap to mind as the go-to clothing of the more socially repressed, angry teenager.

Despite these fairly lame attempts to impose my individuality and snarl in the face of conformity and teenage oppression, I was still a very good, well behaved boy at heart. I never got into trouble at school, except for the breaches of uniform policy and wearing earrings. I would certainly never fail to hand in homework. I could not and would not cross that particular line.

However, in my tiny pea-sized teenage brain there was no correlation between this intrinsic need to comply with the rules and the sort of organisation, planning or forethought required to ensure homework deadlines were met. Consequently, on this particular evening I was left facing the prospect of two assignments being due in in less than twelve hours and having done absolutely no work or any kind of preparation.

I worked literally all night, completing the second one just an hour before I had to leave for school. I remember as the hours ticked by, and my writing undoubtedly became increasingly incoherent and nonsensical, asking myself repeatedly, 'Why did you leave it until now? Why didn't you just do it sooner? Did you think it would all go away? You are such an idiot, Fry.'

As a post-script to that story, if confirmation were needed of what an intrinsically good boy I was, I was later elected as deputy head boy, despite the incongruous jumpers, white socks and earrings. I was beaten to the top job by a good friend of mine, the son of a member of teaching staff. Even in the '80s electoral shenanigans were rife. Not that I'm even remotely bitter…

Twenty-six years later and in somewhat different circumstances, I found myself contemplating comparable issues ahead of my first chemotherapy session and feeling the same sensations of frustration and anger. Patrick's voice resonated around the room, asking me the same questions I had asked my seventeen-year-old self: 'Why have you not prepared yourself for this? How can you not be ready? Did you think it would all go away? You're such an idiot, Fry.'

What little preparation I had done was, I thought, in readiness for a metaphorical 5km fun run. Now the day had arrived I found out Patrick had entered me for an Iron Man triathlon. My training had been wholly inadequate. It wasn't going to be possible to bluff my way through this. I was most definitely not ready.

Admittedly, the issues I was facing were significantly more important than the homework situation I had got myself into twenty-six years earlier. I was not now having to contextualise the complexities of the real reasons for the First Crusade or the importance of primaries in the American presidential election process, but I was equally unprepared for the following day. If only the writing of a few hundred words of drivel would get me out of this predicament as it had done all those years ago. This situation was just a little more serious, and I was overwhelmed by the fear I was now feeling. My fears were not unfounded.

LET'S GET THIS PARTY STARTED

My treatments were to be every two weeks, with the drugs to be given on day 1 after which I would have a two-week 'rest' period. The idea of a rest period was always something that riled Patrick. He hated the thought of relinquishing control of me at any point. He was certainly not going to permit me to have a rest.

'We'll see about that,' was his standard response whenever that idea was muted.

The treatment was then to be repeated on day 15, followed by another rest period of two weeks. This four-week period completes a cycle of chemotherapy. On the twenty-ninth day, the treatment is given again, beginning the next cycle.

My course of treatment was to be made up of six cycles, or twelve treatments over six months, the first of which was scheduled for June 19th. This would mean my last treatment, assuming everything ran according to plan, which evidently it didn't always, would be on November 20th.

When faced with that stark reality, all I could think

about was the fact that the end of November seemed an awfully long time away.

I had asked that my chemo sessions take place on Wednesdays, that being one of the days (Thursday being the other) when I don't have the children. It also worked out that the weekends after each of my treatments were the ones when the Small Frys were with their mother, which seemed, prior to the start of the treatment, the most helpful arrangement.

I would normally do the school run on a Wednesday morning, but Melanie and I agreed it would probably be better for all concerned if the children spent the night before my first treatment with her.

Waking up on the morning of that initial session in an empty house, not having to get the children ready for school or do the school run, certainly made the start of the day easier. However, there was part of me that would have preferred the distraction of having them around and doing those daily chores. It would have reinforced my role as Daddy, a role that was to become increasingly precarious as the months passed. Having to look after the children, and simply having them around, always makes me happy. I could have done with that on that day of all days.

Having the children at home with me on that morning would also have negated the irritation I was feeling with Patrick. From the moment I woke up, having not slept terribly well, he had been running around the house like a caffeine-powered Duracell bunny having a sugar rush. He was like a child on Christmas morning. 'Come on, Fry, get up. Get ready, we don't want to be late.'

'Calm yourself,' I implored him. 'What's got into you this morning?'

'I can't wait to get this started. This is so exciting. I just want to get there and get on with it.'

'You're a sick fucker, you know that?'

He said nothing and just grinned.

For many the precursor to their chemotherapy is a commute to the hospital at which they are to be treated. Adding such logistics is not only physically burdensome, but mentally draining. It's yet another thing to think about. It would also likely require, for most people, the involvement of another person to do the driving, as none of us could predict how we might feel immediately after chemotherapy.

Luckily, I had no such logistical hoops to negotiate. My house was just a ten-minute walk from the hospital. As the weeks and months progressed, I became increasingly glad of that ten minutes. After spending the whole day sitting in a chair in the Sunshine Room, I was, if for no other reason, always grateful of some fresh air. It was also close enough to home to not be a physical strain. Sitting in a chair all day being poisoned can be surprisingly tiring.

Making my way to the Sunshine Room for the first time, armed with a bag of books, iPod and laptop, I felt a real sense of trepidation. I was entering the unknown. The whole thing seemed utterly daunting. There was so much, despite all the wonderful help and guidance I had been given thus far and despite all that I had read, that remained unexplained and unknown. Would the treatment itself hurt or be uncomfortable? Would it make me feel sick immediately? How long would it take? How many other patients would there be?

As we made that short walk Patrick could clearly sense my apprehension.

'Come on, you need to do this. This is the next phase of our life together. I will be there every step of the way.' He took my hand and began pulling me in the direction of the hospital.

I wasn't sure which of these particular statements I found more terrifying. The inevitability of what I was about to do, the fact that this was merely 'the next phase' of my life with Patrick – a life I was already despising; a prison from which I knew there was no immediate prospect of escape – or the inexorable truth that Patrick would indeed be there with me 'every step of the way'.

At the suite, I scanned the waiting area wondering if any of those sat there were also awaiting the wonder that is chemotherapy. I made myself known to reception and, instead of being asked to wait as I had expected, I was shown straight into the Sunshine Room. This rather threw me. I wasn't ready. I wanted a few more minutes to try and manage the myriad of thoughts that were rushing around my head. I didn't want to do it. I felt like a child reluctant to let go of their parent's hand at the school gates for the first time and having to be coaxed into the classroom. But there was no putting it off. I could not prevaricate any longer. The time had come. There was to be no more waiting; I was thrust straight into the action.

In future weeks, this fast-track pass that the occupants of the Sunshine Room possess felt rather like a VIP lane at Disneyland, enabling me to avoid the queues and walk straight in. I always did so with a rather smug feeling of inflated self-importance. Like some z-rated wannabe celebrity I could by-pass the masses and tread my own red carpet only accessible to the more important patients, straight into the Sunshine Room.

'You are such a dick sometimes, Fry.' Patrick's assessment was succinct and to the point. He wasn't wrong.

The room itself seemed to have a very different appearance to the one I had witnessed with Peter. It appeared less clinical, with far fewer chairs positioned around the walls. It was obviously neither less clinical nor less populated with furniture, unless of course the suite managers had telepathically taken on board my observations and decided overnight to reduce the number of chairs ahead of my arrival in order to make me feel a little more comfortable.

I was relatively early, so there were very few other patients there. The nurse I met somehow knew who I was and was clearly expecting me. She was very welcoming and asked me to take a seat. Without even a moment's hesitation I chose the one in the corner where I felt I would be able to keep myself to myself as much as possible. I'm never one for idle chit-chat and somehow this environment, despite the very common bond which must exist between everyone there, seemed somewhere I would be even less inclined to want to participate in such conversations.

I rather nervously and self-consciously began to set up my little den for the day – once, that is, I'd managed to successfully navigate the perils of the adjustable table. It was one of those with legs on only one side, the wheels of which slide under the chair enabling the tabletop to lay across your lap and the height of which can then be adjusted. Having successfully passed initiation test number one, and arranged my paraphernalia on the table, I sat down.

Despite the chair being surprisingly comfortable, I sat rather uneasily. I fidgeted and looked around the room, not at or for anything in particular but simply to try to familiarise myself with surroundings that over the next six months would become my second home. It felt like my first day at a new school, with all the other kids looking at me and asking, 'Who's the new boy?'

Everyone else in the room seemed comfortable in what for them was a familiar environment; relaxed, chatting to companions, reading, knitting. I sat rather uncomfortably, not knowing where anything was or what, if anything, I was supposed to do, afraid I would get it wrong.

Patrick sat on the table with his back to me, also surveying our new environment. 'Told you. It's not so bad,' he said without turning to face me. 'Everyone's having a nice time, all very relaxed, keeping themselves busy. You were making a fuss about nothing.'

Again, our definitions of certain words were more than a little different. 'Having a nice time' and 'relaxed' were terms I would not have used to describe our fellow occupants of the Sunshine Room. He was right about something though. It certainly was not nearly as bad as I had feared.

The nurse responsible for the administering of my first treatment introduced herself and took me through what was to happen, and immediately made me feel much more comfortable.

'How are you feeling?' she asked, very genuinely, as

part of the routine pre-chemo interrogation all patients are subjected to before every session.

'You mean apart from the fact that I have cancerous cells trying to take over my body, there's a thirty percent chance I'll be dead in a year, and you're about to poison me?'

'Yes.'

'Apart from that – great.'

In the seconds it took for that exchange to take place, the tone for my time in the Sunshine Room was set: me being an arse, trying to make a joke of everything in a pathetic attempt to disguise my true feelings and deflect from the stark reality of what was happening to me. The nurse smiled politely, with an obvious and apparently sincere look of empathy, disguising what I am sure she was really thinking: *Bloody hell, we've got a right one here.*

Before I knew it, my cannula was in and the party had begun.

THE MACHINE THAT GOES 'PING!'

Now that I had been successfully attached to my drug-dispensing appendage, I was able to get on with occupying myself while the poison made its way around my body. The first three drugs were attached, dispensed and removed and the next connected without any issue. Each was pain-free, allowing me to get on with some of the many things I had brought with me to fill the time.

Most of that first session was spent writing reports for the children in my class. I was, at this stage, very much in a 'things will go on as normal' mode; therefore, having a distraction-free environment in which to complete this task was most welcome.

I had also made the decision, some days earlier, to start a journal. I had no preconceived ideas or expectations about what this may become. It was simply something for me to do during my treatment. I had thought that keeping a record of my treatment and how I was feeling, both physically and mentally, might be quite cathartic. For once, I was right.

Patrick was surprisingly quiet during that first session. He seemed happy enough to just sit and observe the comings and goings in the room, whilst wallowing in the success of the first stages of his plan to ruin my life. Seeing me in that room, attached to a machine, having toxins shovelled into me, clearly gave him a huge sense of achievement and satisfaction. He would occasionally pipe up, 'Does it hurt yet?' The shake of my head with which this question was met was obviously somewhat disappointing, but the overall success of his mission to date was compensation enough.

The Sunshine Room now felt a far more tranquil place than I could ever have imagined. The other Sunshineistas (those who occupy the Sunshine Room) and I all sat, relaxed in our chairs, busying ourselves in our own unique way, attached to the machines dispensing our drugs.

But one thing I became aware of very quickly were the noises of the Sunshine Room, most notably those which emanated from the machines we were all attached to. Periodically each machine beeped, a high-pitched singular tone, rather like a washing machine when it reaches the end of its cycle or the Monty Python machine that goes 'Ping!'.

That in itself would not have been too intrusive were it not for the fact that at the busiest points in the day there must have been close to twenty machines working at any one time. This resulted in an almost constant chorus of beeps, a barrage of noise that, once I was conscious of, I found impossible to ignore. For a while I sat almost in anticipation of the next beep. The sound emitted by the machine was a signal to the nursing staff to do something with it or to act as a precursor to something else. I never did manage to work out exactly what the beeping meant. I was content with the understanding that beeping equated to someone acknowledging the sound and switching it off.

Often, because the staff were incredibly busy dealing with the collection of cancer-riddled individuals spread out around the room, machines were not always acknowledged as promptly as either I or the machine would have liked. This lack of response caused them to go into 'I want some attention' mode that triggered further, more regular beeping. This, in turn, caused me to go into 'for fuck's sake, will someone switch that bloody machine off' mode. The sound was disproportionately irritating. It was like some kind of torture – if torture is administered while you sit in a nice comfy chair, with Smooth Radio playing quietly in the background, and a very kindly soul coming round periodically during the day to offer you a cup of tea. On reflection, torture may be overstating it somewhat.

Nevertheless, it was very much an affront to my heightened sensibilities. So much so that I was frequently tempted to switch my own machine off when its cries for attention went unanswered, but I was always prevented from doing so by Patrick's warning, 'Don't mess with the machinery, Fry. You'll only get into trouble.'

'But they're doing my head in, even more so than you!' I whispered through gritted teeth.

'Well, that's no good, is it? I shall have to up my game. I can't have anything being more irritating than me.'

The intermittent beeping of machines became the

monotonous repetitive soundtrack to my time in the Sunshine Room. Even now the sound of the washing machine at home finishing its cycle takes me back momentarily to my days spent in that room with Patrick and those bloody machines.

Beeping machines aside, the first part of that initial session was completed relatively quickly and without issue. My problem-free day only lasted until the dispensing of the fourth and final of my drugs had begun, however. The bag containing this last drug looked rather different to all the others. It wasn't transparent as the others had been, and the tube protruding from it that would be attached to me was black rather than clear. I didn't really think too much about it and was certainly not concerned enough to enquire as to why this one was different.

After about fifteen minutes I began to feel a pain in the arm into which this last drug was being dispensed. It began as a stabbing pain and very quickly increased in its severity, to the point where it felt as though a knife had been inserted into my forearm and was being twisted. Although I am pretty good at dealing with pain, and have a relatively high threshold, this was becoming unbearable. I was getting closer and closer to the point where I would have to throw off the masculinity mask, unzip my man suit and admit defeat. As I wrestled with my inner macho self, I could hear Patrick's voice: 'Don't do it. Don't be such a wuss, Fry. It's just a bit of discomfort, stop being so pathetic. Imagine what the nurses will think of you if you tell them that it hurts. You've got eleven more of these sessions to do, so how will you look them in the eye next time if you give in so soon?'

His arguments were very persuasive and convinced me to continue to endure the pain for a while longer, but I eventually had to concede defeat and face the scorn of my companion. I called the nurse over and explained, very apologetically, that the pain in my arm had become unbearable. I could hear the shame and disappointment in Patrick's voice as he whispered in my ear, 'Pathetic!'

I actually felt embarrassed in the same way I would have done if someone close to me had expressed such a view of me. In the absence of any other companion on my journey, Patrick's was the only opinion I had. He was the voice of my conscience and I had disappointed him. It didn't matter even a little bit that I had been shamed by the very thing that had put me in this position in the first place. I was mortified.

The nurse was very understanding and did not make me feel in the least inadequate.

'It's part of her job not to make you feel like a complete loser. It doesn't mean that you're not,' Patrick added.

She explained that this final drug is notoriously hard on the veins. Her view was that it should never be given intravenously, and she recommended I have a central line installed for future treatments. Having the drug dispensed that way would prevent any future pain and damage to the arm. For today, however, the best she could do was try it in my left arm and reduce the speed with which the drug was transferred into me.

Neither of these actions helped. I now had the pain in both arms, and it took longer for the treatment to be completed. I appreciated her efforts to help me though.

After a mere eight hours – even Patrick was getting

bored – my first treatment was finally complete and successfully negotiated. Well, negotiated, how successfully is debatable. It had been a long, seemingly endless and, latterly, painful day.

I had arrived at 9:00am and was unplugged from my machine at just before 5:00pm. I was the only patient left. The other Sunshineistas had popped in, had their treatment and gone home, considerably quicker than me. Some had come and gone in a matter of just an hour or so. This was to become the norm for my treatments.

I was most certainly ready to go home.

Before I was allowed to escape, I was provided with a doggy bag full of boxes of medication to take away – steroids, anti-emetics, anti-gout, anti-indigestion and painkillers. I didn't appreciate at the time that these pills, along with many others that would be added throughout my treatment to help me cope with the huge range of side effects, would become my staple diet for the next six months.

Patrick and I made our way home. He was clearly mortified by the embarrassment I had caused him by complaining about the pain in my arm. He did not want to be associated with me. He walked ahead refusing to acknowledge me, in the way an outraged parent might do after collecting a child from school having been summoned to the headteacher's study to be informed of their offspring's misdemeanours.

Whilst a number of the questions I had at the beginning of the day had been answered – I now understood how the day worked; yes, it did hurt; and no I didn't yet feel sick – I was uncertain as to what happened next. Over time what followed each treatment would become a well-regimented, timetabled, predictable routine of sickness, pain and immobility, punctuated with a few 'good' days...another very relative use of that word that is far from accurate and wholly unrepresentative of the reality of the situation.

OPERATION WEE

Inevitably, during the long, long days spent in the Sunshine Room, I had calls of nature to answer. A straightforward activity I had thought. I had, after all, been peeing for quite a while now, was very accustomed to the procedure and had, over the years, actually become quite adept at it. Patrick, however, had different ideas. Instead of it being the most simple, natural and perfunctory of activities, Patrick's intervention ensured that it became a challenge of Krypton Factor-style proportions. Safely negotiating the treacherous journey from chair to loo, a walk of approximately ten yards, was one that took no small amount of preparation and was undertaken with a degree of trepidation.

My drugs were dispensed via a drip, the bag for which was hung on what is best described as a metal hat stand on wheels. Before embarking on my journey to the loo, I first had to ensure that the tube running from the drip into my body was not in any way tangled with either me, any of the other wires that decorated my personal space, or the chair on which I sat. Being tangle-free would ensure I avoided the classic get-out-of-the-chair-only-to-be-dragged-straight-back-down-again scenario. Apart from the obvious discomfort of having the tube that protruded from me tugged on, and the joy such a misfortune would bring my little furry friend, avoiding the embarrassment of failing this most rudimentary of Sunshine Room activities and thus maintaining a degree of credibility amongst my fellow Sunshineistas was important.

Having successfully completed stage one of Operation Wee and got to my feet, still attached to my metal appendage, I was now faced with the task of negotiating the Sunshine Room version of an obstacle course. Chair legs, tea trolleys, human limbs and, of course, the other patients' metal companions, the legs of which always appeared deceivingly long, all formed part of a Patrick-led conspiracy to make my journey as problematic and fraught with danger as possible.

In order to record and add to any forthcoming humiliation, Patrick was always on hand to provide a running commentary of my exploits. The joy and hysteria were always evident in his voice, like some latter-day Stuart Hall on *It's a Knockout* as he anticipated carnage in the Sunshine Room.

All the other Sunshineistas made the journey apparently seamlessly, without hesitation or concern, whilst I must have looked like a drunk bloke trying to negotiate a slalom on a ski slope whilst holding a broom and wearing slippers after a long night in the pub.

The skills I needed for Operation Wee undoubtedly improved each time I undertook the journey, to the extent that by the end of my treatment I would have confidently taken any new Sunshineista under my wing and happily led an expedition force whilst blindfolded.

One thing that did not improve with time and practice was the issue I faced once I'd reached my destination. Answering a call of nature whilst attached to a drip is like peeing with one hand tied behind your back while chained to a supermarket trolley on a hill.

The practicalities of performing this otherwise stress-free activity aside, there was another consequence of my chemotherapy that even my extensive research had failed to uncover…it turns your pee pink!

One of the nurses had given me a heads up about this most peculiar of side effects and I was rather glad she had as I watched a stream of Pinot Grigio Blush Rosé flow from my body. My pee had never looked anything like that colour before, although there may have been occasions when I was a boy, spending weekends at my grandparents' and overdoing the Cherryade, when it would have come close. Even amongst the huge collection of absurdities that made up my time with Patrick, having pink pee remains one of the strangest things that has ever happened to me.

I DON'T FEEL SICK YET

For the first two days (Thursday and Friday) after that first visit to the Sunshine Room I was surprised by how normal I felt. I wasn't experiencing any side effects from the treatment. My body didn't ache and I didn't feel at all nauseous. What I didn't appreciate at the time was that this was a perfectly normal initial reaction (or lack of reaction) to my treatment.

The drugs I was given at the end of each session included those that staved off the worst of the side effects for the first couple of days. I was also to learn, very quickly, that the feeling of normality and wellbeing didn't last very long.

'How are you feeling?' Patrick asked.

'Surprisingly well,' I replied rather tentatively. Tentatively, not because I was unconvinced by my body's response to my first treatment, but because I was rather surprised by what appeared to be a sincere enquiry about my wellbeing from my tormentor. Despite how comfortable I felt in Patrick's presence, each new conversation still provoked a sense of self-consciousness that I was chatting and passing the time of day with a cerebral fabrication.

My body's apparently heroic stoicism in the face of the Patrick-inspired initial chemotherapy onslaught had left me feeling more than a little smug. I had convinced myself that his attempts to destroy my body had failed.

'Perhaps this whole chemo business is not going to be as bad as I feared,' I continued, somewhat self-contentedly.

Patrick said nothing for a while before laughing, and in a most menacing tone said, 'We'll see.' With that our conversation was over and he was gone.

I stayed at a friend's house on that Friday night and woke in the morning with a very strange taste and sensation in my mouth. My tongue, cheeks and gums felt like they had been lined with a metallic veneer. Every time I swallowed or chewed anything it was as if I was licking a ball bearing. I should be clear that I can honestly say I have never licked a ball bearing, but the sensation I was feeling in my mouth was how I imagine a ball bearing would taste. This veneer was not only preventing me from tasting anything I put in my mouth, it was a constant even when I wasn't eating or drinking.

It didn't bother me unduly. Whilst I assumed it was a consequence of the chemo, I also assumed it would go away. For the moment it was simply a temporary inconvenience, nothing to get stressed or worried about.

As the weekend progressed, back at home, alone, with no children, my body started to display an ever-increasing range of previously unexperienced feelings. Ulcers formed in my mouth, which combined with the escalating metallic sensation prevented me from wanting to put anything in my mouth. The sensation of chewing was just too uncomfortable, and I now had almost no sense of taste, other than metal. I developed heartburn that felt like someone had shoved a red-hot poker down my throat causing my chest to feel like it was on fire. I began to feel a strange aching sensation in my legs and my hands started to tingle. This jamboree of sensations, which was having a rave in my body, was joined by a creeping feeling of nausea.

Around 8:00am on Sunday morning I threw up for the first time. I was still vomiting on a very regular basis some five hours later. At this point I decided to take myself off to the out-of-hours GP clinic at the hospital. The short walk to the clinic was punctuated by me throwing up in the gutter of one of the neighbouring roads.

Although the clinic was relatively quiet and I didn't have to wait very long, I spent the whole time in fear of having to throw up again. I managed to prevent that indignity long enough to be called through by one of the GPs on duty. He was pleasant enough and listened attentively to me telling him about the chemo I had started four days earlier and that I had been vomiting all day. He explained this was a common reaction to the treatment, but if things did not improve I should return later in the evening.

I made my way home, now feeling both metaphorically and literally washed out. Nothing changed. I continued to be sick at regular intervals until 8:00pm. This prolonged vomit-fest prompted me to initiate a conversation with Patrick.

As I sat on my bathroom floor gripping the loo bowl

so tightly I was apparently concerned about the prospect of it taking off, I begged him, 'I can't do this for six months. Please make it stop.'

I had been at this cancer thing for just four days, but was already at the end of my tether, or so I thought. It turns out my tether is considerably longer than I had previously imagined, although with Patrick's help I did get nearer and nearer the end of it as our journey together progressed.

He wasn't terribly sympathetic. 'This is how it's going to be, Fry, get used to it.' He patted me on the back and left the room.

I decided that being sick for twelve hours probably justified another visit to the hospital. So I set off again for the out-of-hours clinic. This time I managed to get there without having to make a pit stop. I saw a different GP. She was delightful, wonderfully kind and supportive, despite the fact that I threw up in the basin in her consulting room. She told me that she wanted to admit me to hospital so I could be placed on a drip and observed overnight. I refused. I couldn't bear the thought of waiting around for a bed to be found. I was so tired I just wanted to sleep. I wanted to go home. Most of all I wanted to stop being sick.

Our consultation coincided with the end of her shift. She explained that she would not allow me to walk home alone given the state I was in and offered to give me a lift. Although I am fairly sure giving patients a lift home is not part of the Hippocratic oath, it was a gesture of compassion I will never forget. The kindness I felt in that moment is indescribable. I have no idea who she was, but whoever you are, thank you.

By Monday morning things had improved a little.

Although I still felt incredibly nauseous, I was not throwing up nearly as regularly as I had been the previous day. I had a prescription for more medication. I have no recollection where I got it or what it was for. I don't think it could have been for any of the drugs I had to take routinely, because they were all provided in a goody bag at the end of each session. It may have been that because Wednesday's session was my first, they provided me with a prescription to collect myself. Perhaps the doctor I saw the previous evening had prescribed me some additional drugs to help with the sickness. Whatever the reason and whoever had supplied it I had a prescription.

I drove to our local supermarket in the centre of town. I stood at the counter of the pharmacy discussing with the pharmacist the fact I was entitled to a medical exemption certificate, which meant I would not have to pay for my drugs, but because I did not yet have one I would have to fork out for this first batch. As our chat progressed and I quickly realised I did not have the energy to argue the toss with him about the funding of my drugs, I suddenly became aware I was going to be sick. I managed to get through the doors before my body took over and I threw up all over the pavement.

As I stood, bent over, hands on knees, peering down at the contents of my stomach on the ground in front of me, Patrick appeared.

'Oh perfect,' I said. I couldn't contain my anger but had very little energy with which to express it. 'Now you're here too. Just when I thought my day couldn't get any worse, you show up.'

'I thought I'd just pop along…' I raised my hand as

an indicator that he should stop and promptly threw up again. Nothing more was said.

It is hard to explain with any clarity or accuracy just how it feels to throw up immediately outside the doors of a supermarket, in the centre of town, in the middle of the day. Most of us have had drunken nights out that have resulted in us pebble-dashing the road or an empty doorway. This felt very different. First, I wasn't drunk and was not enshrined in my alcohol-induced 'I don't give a shit' cloak. Second, it was one o'clock on a Monday afternoon and I was surrounded by people out doing their shopping and enjoying the early summer sun. They were certainly not expecting to have their day ruined by some middle-aged bloke, who could only have been pissed, chucking up in front of them. Fascinated children were moved on at pace by repulsed and indignant parents, while more elderly observers simply tutted and walked on by with a look of revulsion etched on their faces, expressing their disgust that anyone should be that drunk at that time of day.

Stomach duly emptied, again, and well and truly stripped of any dignity, I went back inside to collect my medication and made my way home.

I FEEL LIKE I'VE BEEN HIT BY A TRUCK

Having embarked on my adventures with Patrick I very quickly discovered there is often a considerable difference between the theoretical and written word and the reality of the side effects of chemotherapy.

During our very first meeting, Dr Clark had described the feeling of being 'hit by a truck' as a common reaction to the chemotherapy I was to have. Having managed to get to the grand old age of forty-three and successfully mastered the art of being a pedestrian sufficiently well to avoid a collision with any of the larger vehicles on the road, I cannot claim to know how such an experience leaves you feeling, but I am fairly certain that it's not comfortable. This rather graphic description must, I thought, be consultant hyperbole. It can't possibly be that bad. I was wrong. Much of the time I felt as though the truck hadn't just hit me, it had hit me, and then stopped and reversed back over me for good measure.

For the seven-plus days in the middle of two treatments, the physical symptoms I experienced were unlike anything I had ever felt. In my younger days I had played a lot of sport. I had often experienced the post-match aches and pains common to anyone who plays a physical sport. I had frequently woken up with limbs that would not move and performing even the most fundamental of tasks was made difficult by the immobility of different parts of my body. I had torn, pulled and damaged more muscles than I care to remember, but nothing, *nothing*, came even close to what I felt after my chemo.

For that period between sessions there was almost no part of me that operated or moved properly. Even the smallest of movements was a struggle. Getting out of bed, putting my socks on, showering (not necessarily in that order), making my way downstairs, getting to the loo (thankfully I had one downstairs in the house Patrick and I shared), loading the washing machine and standing long enough for the kettle to boil, all became mammoth feats of strength. Feats that were, on occasion, just too much for me. Such was my inability and unwillingness to move that if you had placed a £50 note on the floor in front of me, I would have had neither the ability nor the inclination to bend down and pick it up.

During my treatment I often questioned why it was that almost everyone I met and spoke to during my treatment, and who was also receiving some form of chemotherapy, seemed to be coping with their drugs far more effectively than me. The more this happened the more I started to believe I was being pathetic and that everyone else was just far more stoic than me. Whilst there may, of course, have been some truth in that, and it was quite possible I was just being more than a little pathetic, I also started to question why my fellow patients and I were reacting in such noticeably different ways.

One particular exchange in the Sunshine Room has stayed with me. I was chatting to the man in the chair next to me, which, yes, I had begun to do despite my initial reluctance to talk to anybody. We exchanged pleasantries and the usual chit-chat before the conversation inevitably turned to our experiences of our treatment. He was a farmer in his late sixties and, like me, was receiving regular chemotherapy, although he was due to have fewer sessions than me over a shorter time frame. At the time of our conversation he was approximately three quarters of the way through his course of treatment. I asked him how he was finding the whole experience, and whether it was having any adverse effects on him. His response surprised me. He explained that since his last session he had continued to milk his dairy herd every day and had dug a ditch in one of his fields. I was surprised because I remember thinking that between treatments I had difficulty pouring a glass of milk or digging in my pockets, and couldn't have dug a ditch if my life depended on it.

I was told by the nursing staff that most of the other older patients were receiving treatments that were less intense than mine because of our relative ages and the likelihood of the treatment ultimately being successful.

Whilst that explanation offered a degree of comfort, it didn't change the fact that my body was utterly useless at coping with the treatment I was given. 'Pathetic' was the word Dr Clark once, light-heartedly, used to describe my reaction to the drugs. She wasn't wrong.

Before my chemotherapy had begun I had hoped, and almost expected, that my body would be the epitome of strength in the face of the onslaught, rather like a tornado-proof building in the path of the deadly winds, defiantly withstanding all that nature can throw at it. I was wrong. Instead my rather flimsy wooden structure surrendered submissively to the bombardment and was reduced almost immediately to kindling. It was indeed 'pathetic'.

When I was able to get my arse off the sofa, I could only walk very short distances before the pain and fatigue consumed me. I got breathless walking from my sitting room to the kitchen.

In the absence of any help at home I still had household chores to perform, mainly for the children. They had to be taken to school. Baths had to be run, and hair washed and dried. They needed feeding and their washing done. The latter task had to be performed while I sat on the kitchen floor to load the machine. Standing and bending to transfer clothes from linen basket to machine was simply too much for me.

They needed me to undertake the Herculean mission of getting up the stairs to kiss them goodnight and read them a story. These tasks, which I had always performed with an enormous amount of enjoyment and love, because they were part of my job as Daddy, became such an exhausting chore that I dreaded them with a passion. It was yet another example of my failure in the Daddy stakes. Patrick was now taking the joy of my children away from me too.

The school run was particularly difficult. Children need to be organised with a patience threshold beyond that of mere mortals. Bags had to be packed. Shoes had to be put on, both mine and theirs. Looking back now, it is comical to think how I must have looked struggling to bend sufficiently to put a pair of shoes on.

Having successfully left the house with three children in tow, I then had to make my way from the house to the car and, once there, ensure all the Small Frys were safely strapped in. Why did so much of my life now involve bending down, and why was my body so unable to perform such a basic task?

Although I was off work, I continued to avail myself of the use of the staff car park. Unfortunately, this wasn't quite as convenient as you might imagine. Getting from the car to the playground involved a mammoth expedition of approximately one hundred yards.

The children all released from their car seats, and with school bags in one hand and a child's hand in the other, we set off. Thankfully, they have always enjoyed school. This enthusiasm meant they were inevitably keen to get there as quickly as possible. Unfortunately, their decrepit old man was not able to maintain the pace they wanted. I often had to pull back on the arm of whichever hand I was holding, restraining them like a puppy on their first walk, trying to persuade them to go at my pace and not theirs.

I rarely allowed the wrecked, decayed me to be seen by anyone other than medical professionals, particularly on my really shit days. In order to ensure no one was subjected to that sight, I always tried to pretend when in public. So the walk to the school gates was not only tiring but a pretence. The extra effort involved in trying to walk normally and hold my body up straight was exhausting. Why I felt the need to pretend, I could not honestly say. Perhaps it was for the benefit of my children; maybe it was for the children I taught, their parents or my colleagues. I didn't want any of them to see me in such a state. Whatever the reason, I tried really hard to undertake the journey to the school gates in something approaching a normal way.

Equally as taxing as the physical pretence was trying to ensure I wasn't physically sick at any point during that two-hundred-yard round trip. The indignity of being observed throwing up outside the school grounds was something I could really do without. I was, with one exception, successful in achieving this goal. As Basil Fawlty might say in true 'don't mention the war' style, I did once, but I think I got away with it.

Having reached the point at which I could relinquish responsibility of Mollie, Libby and Will for a short while, I would hug and kiss them goodbye, tell them how much I loved them, and wish them a good day. Much of these declarations of love and good wishes were lost into the ether. As I spoke, each of my children in turn was getting further and further away from me in their haste to get into school. If I was lucky I got a 'Bye, Daddy!' as they ran off, far more interested in finding their friends or running around in the playground and looking forward to what their day of learning had in store for them than saying goodbye to me, which, of course, is exactly how it should be. I could leave them knowing that a degree of normality had been restored to their little lives, at least for a few hours, in the familiarity, safety and comfort of their school.

It is extraordinary how Patrick's presence had made

just saying goodbye to the children at the school gates such an emotional thing to do. I am not suggesting for a moment that each morning felt like a final goodbye – I was always fairly confident I would still be around to collect them at the end of the school day – but Patrick had heightened all my emotions to ridiculous, off-the-scale levels, and any kind of departure from my children was upsetting. Extraordinary really, because before Patrick arrived, I couldn't wait to get rid of the little buggers!

Reaching the sanctuary of my car was always such a huge relief. I could pause for a moment, take stock and try to regain my composure and ability to breathe. Having successfully delivered the children to the care of their teachers, I often had mixed emotions.

I felt a sense of pride that I had managed to fulfil one of the remaining activities in my not yet completely defunct role as Daddy; relief that I had successfully completed the task without being seen, or at least not being seen as some dilapidated invalid, and I hadn't thrown up. These positive emotions sat in stark contrast to the gut-wrenching (literally) sense of pathetic-ness I also felt.

Although there was a relative satisfaction in doing what I had done, my feelings of inadequacy were shared by Patrick.

He mocked me. 'You're pathetic, Fry. You can't even get to the school gates and back. That's ridiculous. You're forty-three, yet your body's capabilities are akin to those of a ninety-year-old. A rather decrepit ninety-year-old at that.'

Now I was alone again with Patrick, and, despite the mockery of my companion, I could at least abandon the pretence and relax, albeit in a very relative sense. I could drive home and remain there, safe on the Isle of Patrick until it was time to collect the children and do it all again in reverse.

Although passing my children over to the care of their teachers was difficult on many levels, the upsetting nature of it was eased considerably by the thought that I could now go home and go back to bed in peace knowing they were safe and happy.

YOU LOOK WELL

My reaction to being told I had cancer surprised me; or rather the lack of any discernible reaction surprised me. I didn't feel anything. I didn't cry, I didn't feel despair, I wasn't angry. I didn't feel the shock depicted on a MacMillan television advert where the cancer sufferer is shown collapsing upon hearing the news they have cancer, only to be caught by a Macmillan nurse.

Of course, my reaction to having cancer was not limited to the moment when I heard those immortal and unforgettable words. My reaction to, and feelings towards, Patrick changed all the time. From the outset, and for the vast majority of our time together, I was very pragmatic about the whole thing, from having lots of practical questions – What is the prognosis? Is it going to kill me? How can it be treated? How will it affect my life? What can I do about it? – to making the necessary arrangements in the event I became one of the thirty percent.

It was not only my reaction to having cancer that shocked me. The range of reactions from people both when they first became aware of the fact I had cancer, and during the course of my treatment, fascinated, surprised and, in some instances, shocked me.

Some of the responses I received were and are genuinely moving and really touched me. I received a number of cards from children and parents at school containing sincere messages of goodwill, some from people I barely knew, and I was truly moved by the kindness and thought involved in making such a gesture.

Shortly after Patrick and I joined forces and my cancer became common knowledge amongst the school community, a 'Race for Life' was held locally. Amongst those taking part was a girl I taught, who at the time was probably about eleven years old.

She was very keen on rugby and had asked me if she would be permitted to play with the boys. Having a girl play rugby was not something as a school we had ever done before, but I was very happy to allow her to do that. She soon developed significantly as a rugby player, to the extent that I selected her to play for the school's under eleven first team. She was the first girl, in any of the schools I am aware of, to play with her male counterparts. I am delighted she has continued to play rugby, despite suffering significant illness herself, and is playing at a very good level. At the time of writing she had recently made her Premiership debut for Worcester Warriors Women. I am really proud of what she has achieved and would like to think that I played a tiny part in her sporting development.

Each runner in the 'Race for Life' wore a race label for the event. Printed on the label was a speech bubble on which they could write messages relevant to the cause or particular people for whom they were running. She dedicated her run to me by writing 'Mr Fry' on the front of her bib. Such a gesture of compassion and understanding surprised me, particularly from one so young, and was overwhelming. It is something I will never forget.

Just as some of the messages I received were pleasantly surprising, I was almost equally surprised not to receive messages from those to whom I thought I was closer, such as my colleagues at work. I realise the lack of communication was not necessarily because they did not care I had cancer, or that I was embarking on a hideous journey that could ultimately result in me dying. The lack of communication may have been a result of an uncertainty as to what was the correct thing to do/say in such circumstances. Perhaps they simply didn't know what to say to someone who has cancer, an uncertainty that resulted in them doing nothing. This is a commonly held reaction, and if the boot were on the other foot, I may well have been amongst their number.

It may, of course, have been that no one contacted me because they just didn't give a shit.

Some colleagues/parents, when meeting me in the street, would ask 'How are you?' In this context such a simple, everyday, almost throwaway line takes on a completely different social context for both the asker and the recipient. Although there is a genuineness and honesty about the question and the sentiment on which it is based, it is not a question to which, socially, one is expected to give an honest response if such a response is anything other than positive. One is expected to say, 'I'm fine', 'not bad', 'getting there' or simply 'okay' and, for a short time, this is exactly what I did. These positive but untrue verbal responses were usually accompanied by a smile to ensure the asker was sufficiently convinced. I had provided them with the positive response they were seeking, and they could go about their business in the knowledge that I was 'okay' and satisfied they had met their social responsibility in enquiring about my health and thus presenting me with the belief that someone cared how I was.

However, the time quickly arrived when I began to adopt a rather different approach. In a flagrant breach of the well-established social conventions applicable to this situation, I started to provide an honest answer to the question. This invariably made the questioner feel uncomfortable, partly, I imagine, because it is a breaking of the 'rules' which they had not expected, and for which they had no frame of reference for dealing with. Whilst it was never my intention to make the questioner uncomfortable, I had adopted the view that they had asked, and I was no longer prepared to pretend. I could no longer justify in my own mind providing them with an untrue response simply because it was what they expected, and undoubtedly wanted to hear. If they were lucky their question would induce the honest response 'not too bad today' or 'having a good day today', accompanied by a reassuring smile (mine not theirs), and with that we would both go on our way. If, however, they had the misfortune to question me on a bad day they would receive a diatribe, often in some detail, of just how hideous I was feeling at that particular moment. I would happily and unashamedly regale them with tales of sickness, constant pain, mouth ulcers, chronic heartburn and unimaginable fatigue. I used the phrases 'crock of shit' and 'I feel like I've been hit by a truck' a lot.

After thrusting such negativity upon their day in a way they would never have foreseen, I often felt guilty. They had been so well meaning in asking in the first place, only for me to take massive moon steps outside the parameters of social convention and give them an insight into what things were really like for me instead of lying to them.

There will be those cancer sufferers for whom the expected socially acceptable lying will be a godsend; those who have no desire to share the details of the shit they have to go through and who are happy to present a facade of normality and pretence to the outside world. Initially, I was one of those people. I am unsure as to whether that reaction came from an intrinsic desire in me that I did not want people to know details about matters which were so personal to me, or whether there was an element of the English stiff upper lip, carry on regardless and don't show any signs of weakness attitude. Realistically, it was almost certainly a combination of the two.

As a fundamentally very private person, I certainly embarked on my journey with the attitude that I wanted as few people to know as was humanly and realistically possible. It soon became clear that this was not going to happen. More significant was the change in attitude that came about in me.

In a relatively short time of dealing with the shit that Patrick created I got to a point where I was perfectly happy for everyone to know. I was suffering and I was buggered if I was going to do so in silence! I wanted to shout from the rooftops and walk (when I could) around town sporting a t-shirt that said 'I've got cancer. It's SHIT.'

Those to whom I am closer enquired about my wellbeing genuinely wanting to know, and were therefore more receptive to the responses they received, however unpleasant they were.

Undoubtedly people's reactions vary enormously when told that someone they know, whether that person be a friend, an acquaintance, a teacher, a colleague or a family member, has cancer. Some are very inquisitive, express their concerns and desire to help, often quite vociferously – at least initially. However, this enthusiasm to help and to listen quickly wanes as they, perfectly understandably, get bored of hearing about pain, fatigue, vomiting and thoughts of impending doom.

We all want and need positivity in our lives. It is a perfectly normal and natural instinct. Having someone consistently dampening your otherwise positive mood by sharing tales of woe is dispiriting and exhausting. It soon becomes something we will automatically, albeit perhaps subconsciously, try to avoid. People soon get bored of hearing about cancer and chemotherapy. They don't need or want that in their lives. There is a direct correlation between the magnitude of the physical and mental effects of cancer treatment and the unwillingness of onlookers, even those closest to us, to be bombarded with someone else's shit.

Others clearly struggle to know exactly how to articulate their feelings. Some do not do or say anything at all, which is the natural extension of the 'not knowing what to say' group.

Then there is the final group. A group I had read

about but who I never really believed actually existed. It was this group who shocked me the most.

These were the people who deliberately sought to avoid any contact with me at all. There were occasions when people actually went out of their way, i.e., literally crossing the road and pretending they hadn't seen me, to avoid having any interaction with me and thus neatly avoided having to deal with the issue at all. I am as certain as I can be that these actions were not borne out of a lack of care for my wellbeing, but stemmed from an intrinsic inability that many people, English people in particular, have to deal with such situations. They make many of us very uncomfortable and consequently our reaction is to do whatever we need to do to ensure we avoid the situation and the resulting discomfort completely.

During my exchanges with those who didn't manage to successfully avoid me, they would frequently say the three little words that caused me such disproportionate, inexplicable, indefensible rage: 'You look well.' Never before had such an innocent, well intentioned, positive compliment engendered such feelings of fury and the desire to inflict physical violence upon someone as they did in me. It felt like the ultimate kick in the teeth to be told how well I looked when in fact my body and mind were telling me something very different. I felt like shit. I could never understand why that wasn't obvious to anyone who saw me. Perhaps it was, and they were lying to me in an attempt to try and make me feel better. If so, it didn't work. In fact, it had exactly the opposite effect. It created within me a feeling of a lack of understanding and made me feel even more isolated.

Patrick often said it just to wind me up, knowing full well the reaction it would provoke. 'You look well' or 'Looking good, Fry' he would giggle before disappearing, thus denying me the opportunity of ripping his sarcastic little head off.

DADDY, WHAT IF YOU DON'T GET BETTER?

My cancer experience and relationship with Patrick was a very personal affair and one I shared only very reluctantly with anyone else (until now), other than those unfortunate parents who caught me on a particularly bad day outside the school gates. As much as I wanted my association with Patrick to remain a private matter, it was impossible that his existence and his inclusion in my life would not impact on my children.

Undoubtedly, the hardest part of my time spent with Patrick was the effect he had on the Small Frys. After his introduction into our lives it very quickly became evident it was not going to be possible to get through this in anything approaching a subtle or unobvious way. I had to make a decision about what, if anything, I would tell my children.

I believe very strongly in telling my children the truth, even when faced with the kind of difficult questions children can pose. I am not one to shy away from thorny issues. I am happy to discuss and be honest about matters of moral, familial or cultural importance. We have discussed such potential parental banana skins as: 'Is there a god?'; 'Where do babies come from?'; 'How did Donald Trump become President of America?'; and 'What's Brexit?'. Three of these four issues pose not inconsiderable difficulties when trying to explain them to an adult. Attempting to get my children to understand my views on the presence of a higher spiritual being, why Americans had thought it okay to elect an imbecile to become the most powerful man in the world, or the finer points of the UK's escape from the evil clutches of the European Union proved even more problematic. However, they were, nevertheless, issues I was willing to discuss with them.

There are, of course, exceptions to this self-imposed 'I always tell my children the truth' rule. I am very happy to tell blatant falsehoods to my offspring in relation to certain matters, such as the existence of Father Christmas, the Easter Bunny and the Tooth Fairy, plus: 'Yes, we are nearly there'; 'The batteries [in that toy that makes a horrendous noise] have run out'; and 'Broccoli really is so delicious, try it.'

It is easy, or at least natural, to forget, or not to see at all, just how much having cancer affects those close to you. Having given it a lot of thought and in order to protect the children, I decided I would make a conscious effort to involve them as little as possible. However, much as I tried, it was inevitable they became aware that something was going on. Something was different. Daddy was different. They knew I wasn't at work; they inevitably knew when I was struggling; they were aware I had appointments. All of this information accumulated in their young minds for them to process.

How they did that and what conclusions they reached is anyone's guess. I certainly had no idea.

Ultimately, I decided I would tell them I was poorly, but I would not mention the 'C' word. My thinking behind this decision was that given their respective ages – seven, five and four – their only exposure to and experience of cancer in their short lives had been in relation to tragedies that had befallen other families at school. I did not want them to go to school and tell their friends, 'My Daddy's got cancer' only for one of them to say 'My grandma had cancer. She died.'

It soon became very obvious to my children that I was unwell. I was very different to the Daddy they knew before I started my treatment. On my bad days, I found it difficult to move. I certainly wasn't able to play with them, and taking them anywhere was an impossibility. Caring for them in terms of washing their clothes, cleaning and cooking was incredibly difficult. These were the times when I really did wish I had someone around to help me.

My first attempt at addressing the subject of my illness resulted in what must be one of the best examples of the refreshingly simplistic way children see the world around them and their ability to cut through all the crap and tell it as it is.

Once it became abundantly clear that my treatment was making me unwell, after considerable thought, and rehearsing exactly what I was going to say, I addressed the issue with the children. I explained I wasn't very well and that I was going to have treatment which was likely to make me feel quite poorly. Despite the numerous times I had gone over in my head what I would say and second guessing the children's response, what Mollie, who was only seven at the time, said in reply left me literally speechless.

Faced with the news that her Daddy was to be treated in a way that would make him feel unwell, she said, 'That doesn't make any sense, Daddy. What's the point of that? Doctors are supposed to give you medicines to make you feel better not worse!' I couldn't argue with that.

For the most part Mollie, Libby and Will dealt with my illness, and the effect it had on me and them, incredibly well. They were amazingly understanding and showed few signs of ever being upset, distressed or worried about what was happening to their daddy.

I am sure they had concerns, and it is likely they may have discussed these with their mother, but very rarely did they manifest themselves when they were with me. However, the thought of the bravery and compassion shown by my children in order to not upset me was incredibly distressing. It breaks my heart, even now, to think that any of my babies felt upset or worried during my treatment but withheld expressing any such views to me in order not to upset me. It should have been me protecting them from pain and upset, not the other way around.

There were two occasions I remember very clearly when they did express their concerns to me. The memory of their anguish is more vivid than almost anything else about those first seven months. I remember how much their occasional declarations of concern and worry disturbed and shattered me.

After three weeks of treatment – two chemotherapy sessions – we were on our way home from school when Libby became very upset. She was sitting in the back of the car with Will. I asked her what the matter was, but she didn't reply, she just put her head in her hands and sobbed. Mollie interjected, 'I know what's wrong with her, Daddy, because I feel the same.' She then paused, clearly considering exactly what she was going to say. 'What if you don't get better?'

Those six words hit me like a punch to the solar plexus. I had probably always known I would have to have this conversation with my children at some point, but I had clearly diverted it to my subconscious, in the desperate, as it turns out, forlorn hope it would never happen. I pulled the car over, leant across and held Mollie in my arms. I then leant back to try to console Libby, who had calmed down a little, presumably relieved that her big sister had spoken up. I gestured for her to come forward and sit with me in the front of the car.

I held Libby close to me and sat looking at the girls. I had no idea what to say. Will seemed not to be unduly concerned about the topic of conversation as he peered out of the window and munched on a biscuit. Actually, less munched and more broke into as many pieces as possible and spread around the car. He had apparently entered a competition for under-fives to see who could make the most mess in the back of their daddy's car. He was winning.

Mollie had obviously been bottling up these feelings, presumably for fear of me being cross, or because she was worried about what the answer might be, and now as tears rolled down her little face they were finally coming out.

I felt so guilty for causing my beautiful girls so much pain, worry and upset. It hurt me physically to think they had these feelings inside them because of me. Every fibre of my being wanted to tell them it will be okay, that Daddy would be fine. I couldn't. I had always told myself I would not tell the children it would be okay until I knew it would be, and we were an awfully long way away from knowing that. The best I could do was to tell them, 'Daddy is going to keep having his treatment, which will make me feel a bit poorly. Not every day is bad, and you really must try not to worry. I will do everything I can to help the medicines to work so that I get properly better and back to normal.'

There was silence for a moment and reassuring smiles and cuddles were exchanged. The girls seemed to have accepted my response. If only I had been as reassured by my words as my children appeared to be. Precisely how much they really accepted it I don't suppose I will ever know. There is part of me that still believes Mollie was actually thinking, *Yeah, I know that's nonsense, Daddy, and you're still not telling us the truth but thank you for trying.* If that was indeed how she was thinking then that meant she was left, despite my best, albeit ridiculously inadequate efforts, with a feeling of confusion and sadness.

Will had said nothing during this time. I had assumed he was aware of the discussion but had chosen not to contribute. It may have been that he had no interest in the topic of conversation and his mind had wandered to consider far more pressing matters in his life than his father's wellbeing or his sisters' upset; taxing issues for a four-year-old's mind such as Why are leaves green? Where does the sun go at night? and Can Fireman Sam come to our house to play? He did eventually break his silence. 'Daddy?' he asked in a very serious tone, which suggested he had been contemplating for some time what he was about to ask. My heart sank as I braced myself for more heart-breaking admissions and concerns from my son. 'Daddy?' he asked again before pausing, the thought process in his mind clearly evident on his face, 'What's for tea?'

HOW WOULD I SAY GOODBYE TO MY CHILDREN?

As I lay in bed that night, unable to sleep because of the pain in my legs, thinking about what Mollie had said and picturing the expression on her face as she told me the worries she and Libby were feeling, I cried. As I did, I realised that was the first time during my journey with Patrick so far that I had felt any tangible emotion about what I was doing.

Until that point, I had not seriously entertained the thought that my treatment would not work and Patrick would kill me. I had not therefore had to consider the effect that my death would have on my children. Our earlier conversation had forced me to address the thought of dying and me leaving them without a dad.

I had no idea how to deal with these thoughts. What could I do to prepare us all for that eventuality? Should I be preparing us for that at all? Was it something I should discuss with them? Perhaps I should just ignore it in the hope the issue never had to be addressed?

I eventually decided to pursue the easiest option available to me – do nothing and hope it never became an issue. This ostrich approach was most certainly not the most parentally responsible but was the course of least resistance.

I did, however, make one decision based on the possibility of my imminent departure. I booked a photo session for me and the children so they would have some photographic memories of me and them together should Patrick's mission be successful. Even if I was to survive the whole process, I assumed there was a chance I would look very different to when I started. Having the photos taken would mean I could be remembered the way I used to look.

The photo session was great fun, we had a lovely time, and we now have some fantastic photos to remind us that even through such a difficult, challenging and miserable time we were still able to have fun and smile together. Pictures of me and the children smiling and laughing together was the way I would have wanted them to remember me. Booking that session was most certainly one of my better decisions.

A few weeks into my treatment I received an unsolicited call from the local hospice. I was rather surprised to hear from them – did they know something I didn't? Perhaps they were just getting in early? I was surprised that hospices touted for business! I broke off the call momentarily and muted the phone.

'Patrick!' I yelled. 'Is this something to do with you?'

His little furry self appeared in the door of the lounge. 'What?' he replied, the picture of innocence.

'I've got the hospice on the phone. Did you contact them?'

'I actually didn't, but I'm definitely going to make a note to do that in the future. That's genius!' He wandered off, clearly inspired by the information he had just been given.

I returned to the call. Patrick was telling the truth; they had in fact been contacted by the children's GP following a request from Melanie for help and advice on how to support the children with their feelings during my cancer treatment and he had referred her to the hospice. They wanted to ask my view about what, if any, involvement the hospice could have that may benefit the children, and to seek my permission for any agreed course to go ahead. We chatted and discussed the pros and cons for the children of such an intervention. Instinctively, and somewhat defensively, I felt the children didn't need any help other than what I could give them. It is my job to protect my children. I don't need an outside agency to do it for me. That was, of course, utter nonsense, and I eventually had to accept in this case scenario, regardless of how much I wanted to, that I wasn't going to be able to help and support my children – something else that made me feel completely inadequate and a failure as a father. I'm their dad, I should be able to help, support and protect them in any situation. They should always be able to come to me for help. It's my job. However, begrudgingly, I had to concede that for their benefit such assistance should come from a professional. A meeting with a counsellor was agreed at a date to be arranged.

That evening I spoke to Melanie. She raised some concerns about Will's recent behaviour. She also mentioned to me that he had asked her about me 'not being here'. It broke my heart to think about my gorgeous little boy thinking and worrying about the possibility that his daddy might not be around.

At bedtime that night I sat with him, cuddling him until he went to sleep. In fact, it was he who was cuddling me. I was sitting on the floor next to his bed and he invited me to lay my head on his chest, he put his arm around me and stroked the back of my head. I just lay there and cried, again, as I thought about the anguish, turmoil and upset Patrick was causing my little boy and that I was unable to protect him. A four-year-old should never have to think in that way. How does one so young deal with those kind of thoughts in his little head? He shouldn't be dealing with this sort of crap.

Even at such a young age, Will was obviously more affected by Patrick's presence and my struggles than I had perhaps appreciated initially. As well as his expressed concerns, he became increasingly reluctant to sleep in his own bed. The children frequently slept in my bed before Patrick's arrival, but Will became ever more obsessed with checking where I was and not wanting to let me out of his sight. During the day, if I was ever out of the room for too long, he would call out for me, just so I would answer and he would know I was still there. In the night, on more than one occasion I woke up to find him asleep on the landing outside my door, as if he was preventing me from leaving the room without his knowledge.

For the first time I started to consider a worst case scenario and how on earth I would ever be able to deal with having to say goodbye to my children.

WE HAD SOME LAUGHS TOO

Later that week Melanie attended a support group meeting at the hospice. They offered groups and activities for the children and the 'well' partner, i.e., Melanie, and even though she was no longer my partner, it was important she was there for the children. The sessions included other children who also had a parent or carer with cancer.

I thought that for the children, any children, not just mine, this could be enormously helpful. It must help them to know they were not alone in what they were going through.

I was delighted that Melanie had organised this support for the children. The fact that I wasn't involved in the process was a little frustrating, but understandable. I could see that a process, independent of me, would be more helpful for the children. So, they now had a support mechanism in place and Melanie had a support mechanism in place.

The only person who now didn't have any form of support, outside the walls of the hospital, was me.

I accept that was partly my own fault and that I could and probably ought to have done something about it, but I still had a sense of pride preventing me from actively asking for help both in terms of my own support and in looking after the children when I felt I couldn't cope. There was also a deep sense of inadequacy.

A change of mindset was definitely needed, but could not be guaranteed!

Regardless of how shit I was feeling, the children were always the one thing that kept me going. Not simply because I wanted to get through this for them, so they wouldn't have to face a future without their daddy, but to get through it so this whole thing could end, we could get rid of Patrick from our lives, and go back to being a normal family, albeit a somewhat dysfunctional, one-parent family. I hated more than anything the pain, upset, anxiety and worry Patrick's presence was causing them and how helpless I was to address those issues. All my attempts so to do always felt rather pathetic.

The children's relatively young ages, I think, in many ways made it easier for them. In this kind of situation ignorance can be an advantage. Knowing something about cancer and the possible outcomes must make it harder for older children to cope with the cancer of a parent or loved one. My children were too young to have any appreciation of that, particularly as I never mentioned cancer and simply told them that Daddy was being given some medicine by the doctors which would make him feel poorly but also make him better. Younger children are far more able to accept that kind of explanation.

Whilst the girls, particularly Mollie, quite clearly had a degree of understanding about my and our situation, Will was too small to have any real idea about what was going on, other than what the girls told him, not always helpfully.

Ultimately, like most four-year-olds, any negative thoughts Will had were always very quickly forgotten when presented with something to eat and an episode of *Brum*.

The children helped me through my treatment just by being them. They consistently made me laugh and did things and behaved in a way that immediately took me away from the discomfort and pain I was feeling. They were the antithesis of Patrick and, for the most part, I was able to clearly demarcate my relationship with the children from my relationship with Patrick. We did not have to go through the trauma of having the 'this is Daddy's new friend' chat.

They knew about Patrick, but that was the extent of their relationship.

Patrick was a relentless, oppressive presence. He was literally my constant companion. He would sit and read, watch television and listen to music with me. When I went to bed, he came too. Since his arrival, even visits to the loo apparently became a two-man (or rather a one-man/one-bear) job. When I threw up he was there, if I'd had long (or any) hair he would have been holding it back for me, and my daily struggle to put my socks on had apparently become a spectator sport.

Patrick was a cross between a puppy and a toddler, never leaving me alone, always by my side, never affording me a moment's peace or respite from his demands for attention.

Having said that he was fairly conspicuous by his absence when the children were at home with me. It was almost as if he was allergic to them. They were apparently his Kryptonite. Too much exposure to the Small Frys and all his (demonic, in this case) powers would be lost.

Having long considered why he chose to take such a notably different approach when the children were around, one evening as Patrick and I sat in our lounge, me in the armchair, Patrick laid out on the sofa, I asked him: 'How is it you're with me every minute of every day, but I hardly ever see you when the children are here?'

Patrick set his book down, sat up and looked at me. He seemed surprised by my question.

'You may not see me very much, but I'm always here, keeping an eye on you.'

'But why the difference in approach when they're here?'

'I know you think I'm a complete monster, but even I have limits.'

'Do you really?' I asked sarcastically. 'You'll forgive me for finding that a little hard to believe. Do you have no appreciation of the damage you have done and are doing to my children? Everything you do to me has a massive impact on them. That aspect of you being here makes me hate you more than anything else. You can do what you want to me. Give it your best shot, but the children have done nothing. They don't deserve it.'

'I understand,' came his surprisingly empathetic response, which momentarily took the wind out of my sails as I was gearing up to get into full-on rant mode.

I was actually quite glad of his empathy. Although I

had begun my rant and prepared myself for an uncompromising verbal assault, I'm fairly sure I would not have had the energy to have carried it out.

'I really do understand, but that is just how it is and will be until this is all over. You need to accept it and get on with it.'

Although it may, at first blush, appear that just a hint of compassion was beginning to break through my friend's evil, albeit very fluffy, exterior, this apparent generosity and kindness of spirit didn't actually withstand much scrutiny. What my hairy little associate had conveniently forgotten was the damage he had already done to my children in his takeover of my life. The children were innocent victims, the collateral damage from his occupation of their dad.

Even though Patrick was always a mere spectator while the children were with us, come the evening, children's bedtime routine completed, and the house now in a state of relative peace and quiet, he could always be relied upon to re-emerge from his cocoon of relaxation and once again make his presence felt.

He was always there, buzzing around like an insatiable mosquito, constantly in my space, unappeasable in his efforts to suck my very life blood.

Patrick's stay with us meant that summer was generally a pretty miserable one for all of us. Nevertheless, there were, as there always are with the Small Frys, magical moments when, to a greater or lesser extent, we were able to put aside all the hideousness and laugh together.

Children have a wonderful gift of being able to cut through crap and put aside any difficulties, regardless of their enormity, and retain a carefree, innocently myopic view of life. Despite all the hideousness that was going on around them, and because of their unwillingness to allow Patrick to ruin our lives completely, there were some funny, life-affirming, family-affirming moments. Moments of humour and collective enjoyment. We were still able to have some good times during his time with us.

Sprinkles of normality, just the four of us, with no Patrick.

The weather that summer was particularly pleasant, so the children were at least able to play outside. I would open the doors that led from our lounge into the garden, and I could sit and watch them from the sofa while they enjoyed themselves in the sunshine. I sat and observed while Mollie gathered ever-increasing numbers of minibeasts to show me, and the three of them had water fights. I watched Libby set up a shop and Will create a wildlife park with his toy animals.

I remember one particular incident which was affected by my pathetic-ness but was made all the funnier for it.

Mollie decided it would be a good idea to climb a small tree at the bottom of the garden. I had no issue with that; whilst Mollie is not the most physically gifted of my children, I am not one of those parents who prevent their children from doing anything even remotely challenging for fear of them hurting themselves. My view is, if you fall out of a tree you learn a lesson and do it better next time. Although, in hindsight, what would have happened if she had fallen out, I'm not really sure given my almost complete incapacitation. She didn't fall out. What she did do was far funnier than that.

I had watched her begin her ascent but had not given it a second thought other than to call out to remind her to be careful. Parental responsibility complete, I went on doing whatever it was I was doing – maybe reading, listening to music or watching the cricket. The relative peace of the situation was soon broken as I heard Mollie's voice from the garden.

'Daddy! I'm stuck!' I looked out to see my daughter sitting on a branch approximately nine feet off the ground.

'What do you mean, you're stuck?' I called out.

'I can't move my foot. It's stuck.'

On closer examination from my sofa-based vantage point, it was clear that she had got her foot lodged in the join of two branches. With no other adult around and Patrick unwilling to help in any way, it was equally clear that the only way to get her down was for me to get out there and do it.

I did consider how it would work if I was to leave her there to save me having to get up to help her. It was sufficiently warm outside, I could get food out to her via her little brother and sister, and she could pee from up there. It was doable. For a moment this seemed a genuinely feasible solution to this particular problem. But before I committed to this course my parental responsibility kicked in. I couldn't really justify leaving my daughter stuck in a tree! With a huge sigh and whilst muttering sarcastic expletives about how useless my children were, I got up and walked slowly out into the garden.

I stood for a moment, looked up and examined the problem that confronted me. She was most definitely stuck. This presented me with a very unique set of problems. Getting off the sofa and making my way into the garden had been difficult enough. Extricating my child from a tree was a completely different challenge. The only way to solve this particular conundrum was for me to free Mollie's foot and then have her jump down and for me to catch her. I tried a couple of times to liberate her foot but having to reach up to that height and apply any sort of force was too difficult and I had to stop and rest.

After three or four failed attempts we eventually managed to release the foot. Now came the dismount. But I was absolutely knackered. I had to sit down. As I sat on the grass and looked up at my daughter still sat in this tree, we all began to laugh. Having presumably become aware of the hilarity that was occurring in the garden, Patrick had joined us. Even he could see the humour in this situation. He sat next to me and joined me and the Small Frys in our laughter. The ridiculousness of the situation was not lost on any of us. It was a hysterical scene. A father sitting on the grass, beside an imaginary teddy bear, staring at his seven-year-old daughter stuck in a tree, and neither of them able to move from their positions.

After my little break and with a rallying cry, I exhorted Mollie and me into one final effort. I stood and braced myself, arms outstretched toward her. She jumped, I caught her – just. I gave her a hug, we laughed, and I lowered her to the ground. She went off and continued her games with Libby and Will and I made my way back inside. I collapsed onto the sofa utterly exhausted. That was me done for the day. If she got stuck in the tree again, she was definitely staying there.

My children always enjoyed sleeping in my bed, and I would often go to bed to find it had been commandeered by all three of them. On other occasions the freedom of having the bed to myself was gradually rescinded as the night progressed. However, each of the children approached this task in a very different way.

Mollie's approach was akin to an SAS operation – Operation Duvet. She would get in by some kind of stealth, unnoticed by me until the time came for her to annex my bed. She would proceed to take over both the duvet and the space. I would frequently wake up in the middle of the night and find myself teetering on the edge of the bed, while my seven-year-old daughter made herself comfortable.

Will's approach was very different. He was far more direct and much less surreptitious. He would simply climb into bed next to me, lift my arm up, place it around him, snuggle in and go back to sleep. The whole process was over in seconds.

Libby, like her big sister, was also stealth-like in her approach to getting into the bed. But, unlike Mollie, she was content to take up only the space she needed. She was also a very still sleeper and could therefore often go completely unnoticed. However, if I dared to get too close to her while we slept, she would push me away rather disdainfully as if to say how dare you encroach on my space.

At one point during Patrick's stay I had cause to tell Libby the story of the boy who cried wolf. I don't now remember why I felt the need to share this tale with her, but it is a standard, and frequently repeated, rite of passage for any parent and child. Having regaled my daughter with the story in my most earnest 'this is serious' voice and related it to whatever it was she had said or done, I asked what she thought the moral of the story was. Without even a moment's hesitation she said, 'I need to try not to get eaten by a wolf, Daddy.' I didn't have the energy to disagree.

BECAUSE I CAN

During our time together, Patrick removed every semblance of my life as it existed prior to our meeting. He was hellbent on eliminating anything that could be associated with my past. He refused to let me keep anything that detracted from our relationship and our future, mine and his. He took away my ability to fully enjoy my children, my job, my identity, my dignity and my ability to make my own decisions. Like the dictator leading an invading occupying tyrannical army, Patrick took over every aspect of my life. Patrick was Hitler and I was France. The speed with which I submitted to this oppressive force was not dissimilar to that of the French when faced with Nazi occupation.

There were, however, little pockets of resistance which randomly popped up and displayed their defiance in the face of this dictatorial force that now controlled my life. Although it soon became clear that such resistance was not without risk.

One particularly bloody-minded act of rebellion defied any kind of logic and was potentially catastrophic. Freedom is a much vaunted, cherished, protected and valued part of our lives. Patrick had commandeered mine and I wanted it back. I therefore grabbed any chance that came my way to defy him, even if such defiance was short lived and had no positive long-term effect on Patrick's occupancy of me.

From day one of my treatment I had been experiencing excruciating pain in my hand and arm when the last of the four drugs was dispensed. Shortly after my third chemotherapy session it was decided that, to prevent this discomfort, I should not continue to have my drugs delivered via a cannula. A change would allow the drugs to be delivered more efficiently and hopefully reduce the amount of time I spent in the Sunshine Room each week. I was given the choice of two alternatives in the form of two different types of central line – a PICC (peripherally inserted central catheter) or a Hickman line. I had never heard of either.

It transpired that a central line is a form of intravenous access that can be used for prolonged periods of time to administer substances that should not be administered peripherally, i.e., through a cannula in the hand. Whilst the principles for using the different lines are the same, they offer varying advantages and disadvantages.

A PICC is inserted into the lower arm, under local anaesthetic. The line runs up the arm into the chest to a large vein immediately above the heart. The other end of the line remains protruding from the arm.

A Hickman line works in a very similar way, the only real difference being the positioning of the tubes. The line is put in ('tunnelled') under the skin of the chest and into a vein close by. One end of the line is then slid into the vein above the heart, while the other end comes out of the chest.

After both procedures an x-ray is taken to ensure that the line is in the correct place. The line can then be attached to a drip or syringe containing your medication.

What a dilemma. 'How do I choose between two such wonderful ways of further abnormalising my life?' I asked Patrick sarcastically.

'It's a tough one,' he replied, but was apparently giving it some genuine thought. 'Personally, I'd go for–'

'Shut up,' I barked. 'It doesn't really matter; they're both equally shit.'

I opted, for a reason that is not now clear in my mind, for the PICC line. The procedure was arranged in time for my next chemo session.

The day of the procedure had not begun well. Patrick was pissing me off with his constant chattering and his unquenchable desire to irritate me. He was pushing all my buttons. His mere presence was annoying me even more than normal.

As our time together passed, I became increasingly adept at ignoring the annoying little twat who had invaded my life. On those days when his irritating habits were just too much to ignore, I had taught myself to not let him rile me too much. Thus, we managed to live together in relative harmony.

On this particular day, however, my tolerance threshold was at an all-time low, ignoring him was an impossibility, and I felt more riled than I had ever done. It was not an ideal way to begin a day on which I had to undergo another procedure, albeit a relatively minor one.

As always Patrick was there with me in the room where the procedure was to be undertaken.

'We're here again,' he chirped with an unquestionable glee in his voice.

I wasn't engaging with him today, but ignoring him was in no way diminishing his pleasure. He sat and observed with his usual degree of fascination and satisfaction at the success of his work.

The insertion of the line took a surprisingly short time and was relatively painless. Once it was in place, I toddled off to x-ray for the routine check. The results were not what anyone had expected.

'There's been a bit of a problem,' Peter said, in a surprised but not unsympathetic tone, as he examined the x-ray picture.

'What problem?' I snapped.

'The x-ray shows that the line is not in the correct place.'

'What do you mean? Where is it?'

'In your head.'

It took me a few minutes to compute that information. What the fuck! How did it get there?

'The line effectively took a wrong turn and the end of it is now about here,' Peter explained. He pointed to his right temple. 'In twenty-five years of doing this I've only ever known that happen once before.'

Knowing I was so special did very little to quell the anger that was now roaring inside me. My mood wasn't helped by Patrick giggling in my ear.

'It's okay, we'll just take it out and do it again,' Peter assured me.

My ire index was now at incandescent. 'No, you won't. You'll take it out and I'm going home,' I replied, in what was now nothing more than a bloody-minded act of defiance.

If I'd been in a pram and had any toys they would have been flying around the room as I went into a full-on toddler-style hissy fit. My impression of a furious three-year-old would only have been more authentic if I had laid on the floor, kicked my legs and banged my fists on the ground. I was in raging, unplacatable strop mode.

In that instant I was reminded of an experience I had with Mollie in Tesco when she was around three years old. For no apparent reason, she had a proper, apocalyptic, screaming tantrum in the pasta aisle. Despite all my best efforts nothing could mollify (pun very much intended) her. I tried every strategy available to me from my store of parental techniques. I was calm and soothing; I got cross; I pleaded and begged; I even tried the most potent weapon in a parents' armoury in such a situation – bribery and the promise of sweets, if only she would get up off the floor. It didn't work. Nothing was curtailing my daughter's tsunami of emotion.

As my embarrassment levels climbed to atmospheric proportions, I had one more tactic left. If this failed, then the situation was lost. I laid on the supermarket floor next to her, screamed and flailed my arms and legs around. It worked. Almost immediately, peace was restored, and she got up and walked off.

So angry was I about the failed insertion of the PICC line, that I'm fairly certain that even if Peter had taken a similar approach to me as I did with Mollie it wouldn't have worked, although it would have been a sight to behold. He didn't.

The preceding weeks had seen Peter and I build a good relationship and understanding. He had clearly gained an insight into my personality. Even so, I think the ferocity of my reaction still took him by surprise. Although he clearly did not agree with my decision, having witnessed the severity of my response, he decided against trying to persuade me otherwise.

There was a state of tangible anxiety in the room as kind, well intentioned medical professionals removed the PICC line, whilst tiptoeing around me for fear of unwittingly doing something that might provoke the inner toddler to erupt again, spewing toys and anger-filled lava into the room, covering them and their day in tantrum ash and rendering them helpless, forever paralysed under an ashen cloud of toddler Fry.

The tension-filled silence was broken intermittently by the sound of hysterical laughter. The joyous giggles of an invisible Patrick echoed around the room. It was just as well for him that I couldn't see him. I had been pushed too far already and the little shit's uncontrollable delight as he surveyed the emotional carnage of his latest success was more than I could tolerate.

In that moment, if I had seen him I think I would have ripped his little head off. Patrick's joy was unbounded. He could not have been more pleased with himself. It was only 10:00am but already this ranked as a very good day in Patrick's life.

Procedure complete, I left the hospital without saying a word to anyone.

'That was epic,' Patrick chimed as we made our way home. 'You really lost your shit in there, Fry. Well played. I had no idea I'd irritated you that much this morning. God, I'm good!' The pride with which he made this statement was evident.

Although I had calmed down a little, I was still in no mood to engage with him. Patrick on the other hand was still buzzing from the success of his morning's work. He made no effort to suppress his glee as he continued, whilst almost dancing along the street next to me, 'Fancy that line going the wrong way. What are the chances?'

He paused. Clearly there was something on his mind. When he spoke again his tone had changed to one of earnestness. 'I'm a little puzzled about something though.' He paused again. 'Why did you do that?'

'What? Do what? What did I do? I didn't do anything. This is all your doing,' I snapped, no longer able to ignore Patrick's efforts to rile me. 'The line ended up in the wrong place. It happens. Clearly not very often, hardly ever in fact, but it happens.'

'No, not where the line ended up. I meant why did you refuse to have it done again? I don't understand.'

It was a good question, the answer to which was not immediately obvious. Why had I refused to do something that was most definitely going to be of benefit to me and would hopefully result in pain-free chemo sessions going forward? I still had a significant number of sessions to do. Why would I reject the chance to make the whole process a little easier for myself?

At home, hissy fit well and truly behind me, I reflected on the rather odd decision I had made. Although Patrick and I had only been together for a few weeks, it was evident he was already controlling every aspect of every day. He ran my life. I had a say in nothing. But today I had been given the chance to make a decision of my own. The answer to his question suddenly became blindingly obvious.

'You ask a good question, Patrick, but I know the answer. Why did I do that? Because I can!'

I had to endure one more chemo session before I had a central line inserted. Following the PICC fiasco, I decided to go for the Hickman line instead. This procedure was rather different. It involved a small incision being made in my chest and the line fed in from there. This time, thankfully, the process was completed without mishap and the line was successfully fed through my body to the correct destination. Having the line did indeed make life far more comfortable for me as far as the chemo sessions were concerned.

The insertion of my Hickman line was just one of the very visible signs of my treatment. The children were fascinated by Daddy's 'magic tubes', as they became known. Having eight-inch-long tubes sticking out of my chest made it far more difficult for us to have our cuddles in the way we always had. This was something I was able to explain to them, and they understood, but was no less upsetting for all of us. At a time when I needed them more than ever, I missed those cuddles so much.

However, this was not the only issue caused by my magic tubes. It was uncomfortable to 'wear' them. Even the slightest pull on the tubes protruding from my chest was painful. It made sleeping more difficult than it already was. The line also had to be cleaned every week.

On the weeks when I was not being held captive in the Sunshine Room, a district nurse would visit me at home to 'flush my tubes'. Although the nurses were always delightful, sitting with my shirt off on my sofa while a nurse injected cleaning fluid into me was not the most dignified or enjoyable thing I had ever done half naked.

Following one chemo session, a few weeks after the installation of my magic tubes, I got home and almost immediately began shaking uncontrollably. My temperature went through the roof, and I felt very unwell. So great was the shaking that I didn't have sufficient control of my fingers to be able to text anyone to ask for help. After an hour, during which the trembling, fever and general feeling utterly crap sensation continued undiminished, I was left with two options: call an ambulance or just ride it out. Perhaps in order to try and restore my reputation in Patrick's eyes following his disgust at the weakness I had shown when reporting the pain in my arm at my first session, I opted for the latter. The episode eventually passed after another couple of hours, but it did give me a bit of a scare, particularly as I had no idea what had happened.

When I returned to hospital for my next day out in the Sunshine Room, I was asked all the routine questions about how I had been during the two weeks since they had last seen me. This conversation usually involved reference to nausea, vomiting, heartburn, pain and diarrhoea/constipation. This week I had a new medical issue to throw into the mix. I explained what had happened after the previous session, not expecting any particular response, and was rather taken aback by the telling off I received. I had not been admonished in such a way since I had been an utterly terrified eight-year-old discovered in the corridor of my junior school without permission during playtime by an irate headteacher.

The nurse told me that the symptoms I had experienced were most likely indicative of an infection in my line. Such infections, given the proximity of the line to the heart, can be very dangerous and even fatal. I was told in no uncertain terms that if that ever happened again I was to let the hospital know immediately. Feeling suitably scolded, with the nurse's reprimand ringing in my ears, I settled in for another day of fun and frolics in the Sunshine Room.

Towards the end of that session the same symptoms began to present themselves. Despite the very clear message I had been given at the beginning of the day, I did my utmost to hide the trembling and the discomfort from the nursing staff, for fear of what they might want to do if they found out. I failed. A consultant was called.

I had not met this doctor before, but he was very pleasant and explained the seriousness of what was happening and the potential consequences if it went untreated. The course of action he proposed included me being admitted to the hospital for an overnight stay so that the tubes could be flushed and I could be observed.

Stroppy toy-throwing toddler Fry suddenly reappeared. I refused to stay. I acknowledged the doctor's advice and told him I would happily sign a declaration that I had received and understood the advice but was choosing to ignore it. I was anxious that no one should get into trouble should I go home and my health decline further.

'You're a bloody idiot, Fry. You are so stupid.' Patrick appeared in order to offer his opinion. 'Why are you being so stubborn about this? You do know this decision could kill you?' he asked, knowing full well that I was fully aware of the potential consequences of my decision.

His incredulity was matched by that of the doctor, who expressed very similar views and asked very similar questions. Although I don't recall exactly what he said, I am sure he did so in a rather more compassionate and sympathetic way than Patrick had. The degree of empathy he showed was admirable given the stupidity with which he was being confronted. Eventually he gave up, having done everything humanly possible to have me admitted and treated. He did, however, get me to concede that I would ring for an ambulance if, having got home, the situation did not improve.

On our way home, Patrick was absolutely livid.

'I don't understand why you're being so arsey about this. I thought it was your objective to see me suffer?' I asked.

'It is, but this is not how it's meant to be. If you're going to die it will be because of me, not because of your stupidity,' he shouted. He was burning with rage.

'We'll see,' I replied, whilst suppressing the laughter that I wanted to let out in response to Patrick's reaction. I felt a tangible sense of triumph.

Within a few hours of getting home the symptoms had passed without recourse to an ambulance and admission to hospital. Only after I began to feel 'normal' again was I able to reflect on what had happened and realise just how incredibly stupid I had been. I had ignored medical advice and knowingly put myself in a position that could have killed me. Stroppy Fry had taken the view that 'if it kills me, it kills me'. Patrick could do that anyway. At least this way it would be on my terms.

I could hear Patrick's voice in my head again. 'Why did you do that?'

The answer, just as before, was simple: 'Because I can.'

Regaining any sense of control of my life was becoming increasingly important to me. Such opportunities presented themselves very infrequently but, when they did, I grasped them with both hands, even when doing so was beyond stupid. The feeling of, albeit temporary, liberation from Patrick's tyranny was exhilarating and most certainly worth the risk. It gave me a feeling of possession, of ownership of my life again. Something I very rarely felt during Patrick's occupation.

THANK YOU, SKY SPORTS & TEST MATCH SPECIAL

The summer of my chemotherapy saw seismic changes in my life. Patrick's arrival changed my outlook on life, my perception of others, my priorities and me.

Amongst all the massively significant changes that my adventures with Patrick brought about, there was one which undoubtedly changed my life forever; a change so enormous that I still feel the effects of it every day even though Patrick has long since relinquished his control over me, my body and my life.

Once I became aware of what that summer had in store for me, I made a hugely significant, life-altering, things will never be the same again, decision. I got Sky Sports.

I have always loved sport and, in my younger days, was a keen participant. As my life slid inexorably into middle age, I found myself resigned to the fact that I was not going to fulfil my dreams of scoring a hundred for England at Lord's, playing football for West Ham, or donning a white shirt with a red rose and running out to the strains of 'Swing Low Sweet Chariot' at

Twickenham. I had made peace with the fact that my sporting exploits, victories and defeats were all now to be lived vicariously through the lives of those who actually possessed some ability in the sporting arena and were to be viewed through the miracle that is the television screen.

However, more and more TV sport was now being broadcast exclusively via Sky Sports. I could no longer watch cricket test matches on the BBC, and live Premier League football matches were inaccessible to me. My decision to not purchase Sky prior to that summer had been purely financial: I could not, I told myself, justify such an expense on my teacher's salary. However, the news that Patrick was coming to stay caused a rather drastic change of heart. *Fuck it*, I thought. *So we won't be able to eat for a while; but it'll be worth it.* At least I'd be hungry sat in front of a television that offered me a ridiculous choice of channels and enabled me to indulge my love of sport twenty-four hours a day. It's only money and if I was going to spend the summer sat on my arse I might as well do so watching something I actually wanted to watch. Something to distract me from the pain, fatigue, nausea and boredom of it all.

That decision was undoubtedly up there with the best I have ever made. Having access to all the sporting wonders that were now available to me through the press of a button on my remote control gave me a much greater choice of activity for those long hours spent on my sofa unable to do anything other than read, listen to music and watch the television.

I did read, a lot. I also listened to a great deal of music, but both those activities involved a degree of physical exertion – holding a book in a position where I could read it and turning the pages and having to get up to change the CD. Such mammoth feats of strength and stamina were often beyond me. The television, however, could be watched in a state of complete inertia.

My summer with Patrick was, as luck would have it, an Ashes summer. The Ashes are the epitome of sporting excitement for any England (and Australia) cricket fan. For seven glorious weeks I was able to watch the test series unfold. The England cricket team was led by captain Alistair (now Sir Alistair) Cook, ably assisted in his efforts to retain the Ashes by some of the cream of English cricket – Ian Bell, Graeme Swann, Kevin Peterson, Jimmy Anderson and Stuart Broad. These guys were my constant companions, with the exception of Patrick, of course, throughout that summer.

Their exploits in their battles against their own formidable, ruthless and unforgiving foe became my focus during the first half of my treatment. Without having even the slightest inkling of their importance, Alistair Cook and his players provided me with a distraction and even a purpose. On test match days, the fact that the cricket was on meant I had a reason to drag myself (almost literally) downstairs to the lounge where I could watch these sporting icons in the pursuit of their goal.

An Ashes series is a strange metaphor for cancer treatment. Long days, some rather painful, some spent sitting around rather frustratingly not being able to do anything to contribute to or affect the proceedings being played out in front of you. You struggle and endure for days only to get to the end, sometimes victorious, sometimes utterly defeated, sometimes without any result at all, everything the same as it was when you started. There will be days when you anticipate and look forward to a good day's play, only for the weather to literally piss on your parade. Instead of an enjoyable day spent doing something you love, a factor completely out of your control comes along and takes all that potential pleasure away from you. Whatever the outcome, you know that you are going to have to do it all again in a week's time. You will resume your battle with the same foe in the hope that at the end of the numerous battles you will have fought hard enough to have won the war.

Alongside Sky I would listen to Test Match Special (TMS) on BBC Radio. Not only was the TMS commentary incredibly informative and brilliantly entertaining, it also provided me with a background of wonderfully fond memories.

Commentating on cricket is an art form like no other. Great swathes of a day's cricket are filled with significant stages of inactivity. These periods between overs and even between balls must be filled. The skills of the TMS crew are second to none in doing that. Their observations, critique and reminiscences fill the airwaves like a grandfather regaling his grandchildren with tales of wonder and astonishment of a life 'when I was a boy', or an expert entrancing her audience with the depth of her knowledge and expertise in her chosen field. I am very rarely happier than when listening to TMS.

I am sure I am not alone in using a considerable amount of my time post 'you've got cancer' to reminisce. Time taken to reflect on people, places and experiences in my life, often those many years prior to my introduction to Patrick.

As a child I had spent many a happy hour with my grandfather listening to TMS. My grandfather was blind, so although the cricket was available on terrestrial television in those days, TMS provided him (and me) with an insight and understanding of what was happening at the cricket and enabled us to enjoy a shared passion. Permitting the presenters of the day – Henry Blofeld (Blowers), Brian Johnston (Johnners), Christopher Martin-Jenkins et al – into our garden allowed my grandfather and me to escape to Lord's, The Oval, or one of the other test match venues around the country. We were taken there by the musings of these wonderful broadcasters.

Blowers, Johnners and CMJ are sadly no longer part of the team, their places in the batting line taken by the current crop of commentators (commentators is such an inadequate word to describe the TMS team; they are so much more than commentators) including the marvellous Jonathan Agnew, Simon Mann, Vic Marks and, following his retirement from the game, Graeme Swann.

Listening to TMS still enables me to be transported to a vast array of cricketing stadia around the world and allows me to reflect on a different time, long gone, but much cherished: happy times spent with my grandfather sat together in his garden listening to the cricket. So, during Patrick's summer, the TMS team was not only a very welcome distraction, but a source of great happiness and nostalgia.

Watching Cook, Bell and Peterson take on the Australian bowlers while Swann, Broad and Anderson strove to take wickets, and listening to the TMS team provide the soundtrack to that Ashes series, gave me enormous pleasure and a purpose during that otherwise lost summer. I will always be grateful to them for that. If this was to be my last Ashes series, England's 3-0 victory made it even more satisfying.

THANK YOU, DROITWICH SPA LADIES FC

My own sporting endeavours, if you can call them that, also provided me with significant relief throughout my treatment.

I continued to make my own small contribution to real life sport by continuing my role as coach and manager of Droitwich Spa Ladies Football Club. Although it was frequently very difficult to attend and actively contribute to training sessions, and matches became increasingly hard to be part of, fulfilling that role played a hugely important part in providing me with a distraction and a purpose during my time with Patrick.

The success of the team in winning our league that season was so much sweeter for me, coming as it did just two months after I was told I was in remission. As our penultimate game of that league-winning season was coming to an end, and it was clear that the championship would be ours, everyone around me – the substitutes, other players not involved in the match, and our supporters – were all buzzing around eagerly anticipating the final whistle that would be their cue for ecstatic celebrations. My emotions were also running high, but manifested themselves in a rather different way. I took my seat in the dugout, put my head in my hands and tried to choke back the tears I could feel welling up inside me.

I have always been an emotional coach. I put my heart and soul into working with all the teams I coach, and take all the results, win, lose or draw, very personally. But this team of ladies meant so much more to me than any other team I had ever worked with.

Coaching that team was the most enjoyable experience of my coaching career. Managing that group of girls was not always easy, far from it. Sometimes it was a complete pain in the arse. Dealing with strops and sorting out inter-team relationships, of which there were many, were just two of my many roles. I often felt more like a relationship counsellor or their dad than I did their manager. It was regularly challenging and frequently exhausting, but I loved it.

In the minutes toward the end of that particular match, I was overwhelmed by what we had achieved, how difficult it had been, and just how important that group of players (and my assistant Mark Solloway) had been to me during my treatment. Coaching and managing that group of players gave me a weekly day pass from the Isle of Patrick, although such passes were only provided with very specific conditions – it was valid for one day only and Patrick would accompany me at all times.

My players and Mark were always incredibly supportive, but had also respected my desire for us all to just carry on with things and the workings of the team in as normal a way as possible. Treating me as Ian Fry, gaffer, and not Ian Fry, cancer sufferer, meant an awful lot to me. Working with Droitwich Spa Ladies FC was just about the only place that I could continue to be my pre-Patrick self and I liked it.

I continued to coach the team for some years after my treatment, and we had a number of other successes, but eventually the emotion of being responsible for that group of players and the effect our losses and poor performances had on me personally, and indirectly on my children, became too much and I stepped down. Long after he had disappeared, this was another of Patrick's legacies. Being coach of Droitwich Spa Ladies FC will always be something I look back on with very fond memories and no small degree of pride.

I SPEAK FLUENT CHEMOISH

Chemoish – *Noun* –
the unique language of the Sunshine Room
spoken only by those undertaking chemotherapy.

One thing that became clear to me during my regular visits to the Sunshine Room was the unspoken but nonetheless tangible understanding that existed within the room amongst the Sunshineistas. The understanding that we all – whatever our age, gender, background or medical history – had one thing, one terrifying, all encompassing, potentially fatal thing in common: cancer.

Despite this very obvious commonality, the subject was spoken of only very rarely. Patrick was the bloody huge elephant in the room. His presence was acknowledged through the enormous amount of sympathy that radiated, silently but tangibly, from the room's reluctant inhabitants and their companions.

Each understood, in a way that no one else could, including the wonderful nurses in whose care we placed ourselves for each treatment, just how horrific the ordeal we shared was.

A unique language was spoken in the Sunshine Room. A language spoken by only a select, but ever-increasing group of people whose common experience enabled them to partake in and share a language incomprehensible to those outside the confines of the Sunshine Room.

Chemoish is a language whose key vocabulary is taken from English but would pose a not insignificant challenge to even the most gifted linguist. The primary use of Chemoish relates to a small subsection of words and phrases rarely spoken outside the Sunshine Room, at any time, in only a limited number of other contexts, and very rarely in public. Words which those of us who are fluent in this language use freely and without compunction in our own unique microcosm of life. Words such as constipation, diarrhoea and vomiting are banded around and discussed openly without a second thought. Other utterances, which in any normal circumstances would be used rather more circumspectly in polite company for fear of causing alarm or to prevent embarrassment, like chest pain, breathlessness, infection and hair loss, for example, are used in such a dismissive way so as to almost challenge the meaning and the effects of the conditions described: 'I've had chronic pains in my chest'; 'I get breathless walking up the stairs'; 'I've lost even more of my hair.'

An understanding of Chemoish has only a limited shelf life in the library of our brains, however. Much like school level French, no sooner do you stop using it on a regular basis than your knowledge of Chemoish simply falls out of your head to be replaced by far more important information.

Patrick forced me, and all partakers of chemotherapy, to develop an understanding of and access to certain very specific medical terminology. Like a group of entry level medical students, we all became utterly au fait with the names, and alternatives, of all our own numerous drugs, both the poisons with which we were filled during each session and the myriad of 'takeaways' provided to be taken home and consumed routinely.

This newly acquired knowledge and vocabulary is then used with such confidence and apparent expertise that the casual observer mistakenly finding himself in the Sunshine Room would be forgiven for thinking he had stumbled across a strange pharmacists' convention.

I'VE DONE A POO

Intense relationships can make any of us behave in ways we wouldn't otherwise. During my time with Patrick I became obsessive about many things, things that prior to our meeting I would not have given a second thought to. The flames of obsession sparked by Patrick were fuelled by the fact that I wasn't working. This inactivity, both physical and mental, provided me with an opportunity to think about many things in a way I didn't previously have time to.

I became obsessed with my temperature and weight. I bought both a thermometer and set of scales to enable me to keep a record of the state of my body on an almost daily basis. I had been told that it was important to regularly assess my temperature. A fever can be indicative of a serious issue in anyone undergoing intensive chemotherapy – even though I chose to ignore this at times in my bid for misguided independence. I was also told to keep an eye on my weight and ensure that it didn't drop significantly. Given the amount of crap I ate during my treatment that was never very likely. There can't be many people who put on weight whilst having chemotherapy. I did.

Bowel movements also became a major focus for this particular rather bored teacher during the many hours of silent reflection. All primary school teachers are acutely aware of the power and significance of poo, in both its written/spoken and physical forms. For those teaching the very youngest children, poo can become an all too real a part of the normal working day. For those of us who have fewer concerns about one of our children soiling themselves in the middle of a lesson, poo is a wonderful way to engage with your class. I challenge anyone to stand in front of a class of under elevens and utter the word 'poo' without making the whole group dissolve into uncontrollable laughter. So powerful is this word that it should form part of teacher training. The use of the word 'poo' has an almost magical effect on any group of primary school children. 'Poo' will cast a laughter spell and create hysteria in any primary classroom. That and the word 'bottom'.

Patrick engendered in me an interest in my bowel movements I had never experienced before. I had never imagined that such mundane everyday perfunctory experiences and routines would take on such importance and significance. I had never envisaged a time in my life when I would almost literally celebrate doing a poo.

My obsession with my colonic shenanigans reached levels that would have made even Sigmund Freud's head spin. I had read that chemotherapy can cause both diarrhoea and constipation; not, I had assumed, at the same time. I had not initially given that particular side effect any real thought, given the other potential delightful consequences of my treatment. However, it did not take long before my obsession started to develop. My lavatorial habits fluctuated between chronic constipation and 'the world just fell out of my arse' diarrhoea. This intestinal rota that Patrick dutifully put together for me continued throughout the six months of my treatment. I never got to see the rota. Changes in the schedule were always unannounced and came as something of a surprise.

The constipation was not only incredibly uncomfortable, but also created in me a disproportionate reaction when the time came for it to end. After several days of inactivity in the bowel department, finally managing a poo was the cause of significant celebration.

I felt like my children used to when they were much younger and pooing was apparently a team game. The times I had spent at home minding my own business when a celebratory call would come from one of my children from somewhere in the house – and I just had to pray it was from one of the loos – in a tone that smacked of a combination of joy and achievement, the two words that all parents dread and frequently pretend they don't hear in the hope that the other parent will step up and respond – 'I'm finished!'

That was how I felt when the time came for me to end the latest period of constipation. Although I don't recall ever actually shouting out, I would record the fact that my bowels had moved in my diary and had an almost overwhelming compulsion to tell anyone who showed even the slightest interest in my health. I resisted the temptation to wander the streets or stand on the school playground informing passing strangers that I had managed to have a shit, but I did tell my nurse when I next visited the Sunshine Room.

Each treatment session began with a little quiz. I love a quiz. Thankfully the questions were not the most challenging – the mental state I was in for a significant part of my time with Patrick would have made responding correctly to even the most straightforward of questions a challenge.

'How have you been since we last saw you?' the nurse would ask, pen in hand ready to record my response.

'Ooh, I know this one,' I'd think to myself, desperately searching the deepest recesses of my brain for the answer.

'Come on, Fry, you know this, we've practised this,' Patrick would say, making a gesture with his paws that was presumably intended to illicit some kind of recall.

My mind was blank, however. I could not find the answer we'd rehearsed. Patrick and I would prepare for this fortnightly scenario. He would often appear and fire random questions at me while he chased me around the house like some demented Bradley Walsh.

He would catch up with me in rather bizarre and challenging situations – on the school run, whilst I was on the loo – and on one occasion even decided to ask me 'What is the capital of Ecuador?' while I was on my knees throwing up. He got rather short shrift that day. Mainly because I didn't know the answer!

Patrick's questioning would frequently be accompanied by his own inimitable form of encouragement. 'You need to be alert and focused, Fry. You know what these nurses are like with their general knowledge questions, always trying to catch you out. Come on, focus!'

'Give me a break. It's not bloody *Mastermind*, and even if it were I think I would be okay with my specialist subject, The Life and Times of Ian Fry. Even I might get a couple of those right.'

'Are you sure?' Patrick muttered sarcastically.

Whilst I appreciated Patrick's desire to ensure a problem-free pre-chemo inquisition, his methods, as with all things, left a little to be desired.

Come our next session I was prepped and ready to answer questions on my own specialist subject, so 'How have you been?' threw me a little. I had become accustomed to answering the same specialist subject questions at the beginning of each session. Can you confirm your name? Easy. What is your date of birth? Got that one too. The nurse now threw in this curveball, 'How have you been?' which was not what I was expecting. I had to think quickly, panicked and blurted out the first response that came into my head.

'I had a poo,' I answered with a smile and a justifiable sense of pride and achievement, for both having found an answer to the question and for having defecated successfully.

This comeback was inevitably followed by a sense of indignation when I didn't get the magnitude of response I had hoped for or that I felt my tumultuous news merited. Surely, I should have received some kind of acknowledgement, verbal or otherwise? Perhaps a sticker with the inscription 'I've had a POO!' and a big smiley face on it. Unfortunately, NHS budgets apparently do not stretch to rewarding adults for having a shit.

The nurse clearly did not share my sense of achievement.

'Okay,' came the very underwhelmed reply, although she did write it down, which was recognition of sorts. It was on my records: 'Week four – Ian has done a poo.'

My guts frequently went from the sublime to the ridiculous. Periods of constipation were often followed by episodes of diarrhoea. This was less uncomfortable than the constipation and usually lasted for less time. However, the significant downside, not that there are many positives to having diarrhoea, was that it meant frequent, often very frequent, visits to the loo. This in turn involved me having to get my arse off the sofa, a situation not without its difficulties. On my D-Days (Diarrhoea Days) I considered taking my duvet and radio into the loo and setting up base in there. Camping out in the loo would have saved me the enormous effort of the all too regular trips to the smallest room in the house and, in case my body didn't allow me to get there quickly enough, significantly reduced the very real possibility of me shitting myself and decorating my house with a faecal Jackson Pollock.

Thankfully, things never got quite that bad, no Camp Loo was ever needed, and my clothes and house remained unsoiled.

YOU GOT AN A MINUS

Patrick was my constant companion, always there to remind me of the wretchedness of my situation. I felt like Charlie Brown with my own personal cloud. Wherever I went Patrick accompanied me, but no umbrella of fortitude, resilience or positivity could protect me from the misery he poured down on me. Patrick was my unique dispenser of precipitation. Casting a permanent shadow over my life.

As well as the blocker of light, he filled many other roles in my life. He was my harbinger of misery, my doom-monger, soothsayer, critic, motivator and guide. He juggled all these roles with the dexterity of the most skilled circus performer, undertaking each one with equal skill, determination and no small degree of panache. He took his roles very seriously.

The negativity that surrounded the vast majority of his functions was balanced, to a varying degree, by the more playful side of Patrick's personality. He was frequently mischievous, occasionally funny, and sometimes even convivial and good company.

Whatever mood he was in, one thing could be guaranteed. He was always a presence.

During one session in the Sunshine Room, having got bored of eavesdropping on the conversations of the other Sunshineistas, doing knee slides across the mirror-like floor, or undertaking an obstacle course in which he travelled under and over the unoccupied chairs in the room and in and out of the forest of coat hanger legs and wires, he plonked himself down beside me.

'I'm bored, Fry.'

'What, exactly, do you suggest I do about that?' I responded.

'I don't know.' He paused to give my response some serious consideration, clearly having not given the ways in which I could entertain him any thought prior to that moment. He was presumably expecting a rather less positive response than the one he received. A less positive answer was exactly what I had intended to give him, but I had evidently not been clear enough.

'Let's play I Spy,' came his enthusiastic suggestion.

'No.'

'Rock, paper, scissors?'

'No.'

'My granny went to the supermarket...'

'No!'

'What about 'Would you rather...'?'

'I'd rather be anywhere else than here with you right now!' I'd had enough. The wafer-thin ice that Patrick had been skating on all morning had finally cracked under his weight. 'Please be quiet, you're doing my head in.'

For a moment Patrick adopted his 'you're so mean

to me' face before his attention was caught by the folder that lay on the table in front of me.

'This looks interesting. Can I have a look?' He didn't wait for a reply, and before I could say 'No!' he had picked up the folder in his grubby little paws and begun his perusal of my medical notes. His impression of Dr Clark was quite convincing. He then scoured the pages for some considerable time, giving the distinct impression he had fully understood the charts, test results and comments he was reading.

'You okay there?' I asked after a short period of silence.

'Very good, very good,' he said, nodding his head approvingly.

'What is?' I asked, not for the life of me knowing what he could possibly have found within the pages that would have led him to such a conclusion.

He looked up from his reading and delivered his considered medical opinion. 'You are clearly doing well.'

As much as I wanted to simply ignore him and not indulge his antics any further, I was interested to know what I had apparently done to deserve such a positive assessment. Positivity had been rather thin on the ground, and I was keen to grasp any that might come my way, regardless of the source. I asked rather reluctantly, 'What are you basing that on?'

'They've given you a good mark.'

'What?' I was now starting to lose patience, again. 'What are you talking about, 'a good mark'?'

'They've given you an A minus.'

I shook my head, utterly bemused by this whole conversation.

'It's here. A minus!' He was becoming exasperated by my lack of understanding. He turned the folder round so I could see and pointed to the large letters at the top of the page: 'A neg'.

'That's not a mark! That's my blood group! A negative!' My irritation was transcended by the amusement I felt at my idiotic little friend's error.

'Oh. Yes. Of course it is. Actually, that makes more sense,' came his rather embarrassed reply as he absorbed the ridiculousness of his mistake. Despite his obvious discomfort at having been made to look so foolish, he was very soon back on the 'let's undermine Fry as much as possible' wagon and, in an attempt to regain his position of superiority over me, very calmly and cuttingly said, 'I thought that was high. There's no way you're that good at this.'

As usual Patrick had had the final word and the conversation was over.

When he wasn't making a general nuisance of himself or taking on the role of my physician, Patrick would sit on the windowsill and peer out through the vast window of the Sunshine Room. As well as the other wings of the hospital, car parks and patients, visitors and employees going about their business on the footpaths below, the Sunshineistas could also enjoy the vision of the beautiful Worcestershire countryside disappearing into the distance. As our time together moved on, Patrick's panorama was becoming increasingly limited by construction work being undertaken.

He was particularly upset by this intrusion into his vista from his vantage point.

'Every time we come here more and more of my

view is obstructed by this building work,' he shouted across the room, with no small degree of exasperation.

I was not even remotely inclined to respond to his whinging. It made little difference. He continued his rant.

'So, I'm forced to come here and spend the best part of a whole day in this hideous room every two weeks, with only you for company.' He pointed at me rather dismissively. 'Everyone here is so rude. No one will even acknowledge I exist.'

I wonder why that is, I thought, still refusing to engage with him.

'And the one thing about the day I actually enjoy, apart from analysing my plans for you being executed so perfectly, of course…' – the tone of his voice became more excited as he reverted to his usual sadistic self. 'The only thing I enjoy is sitting here taking in the view, and they're putting a new building directly in my line of sight. Now what do I have? Nothing! At least you get your own chair.'

I felt I needed to say something, for no other reason than hopefully a response might actually shut him up.

'It is shocking, isn't it. It's almost as if the hospital authorities weren't considering the views of a cuddly, school uniform-wearing figment of my imagination when they made the decision to build a new oncology centre for the whole of the county.'

'I know. You'd think the bastards would…' He paused while he absorbed the sarcasm with which my retort had been delivered. It also took a while for the information I had imparted to filter through to his fluffy little brain, but once it had, it clearly pleased him. His frown was replaced by a smile. 'So, it's a new oncology unit? Excellent!'

The realisation that the structure being erected before his very eyes and ruining the view from his second-floor observation platform was being readied to house an army of new cancer patients visibly changed his opinion from frustration and anger to one of delight. This was no longer an eyesore. It had become an opportunity. A new challenge.

I HADN'T DONE THAT SINCE I WAS ELEVEN

As a child I was a bed-wetter. This relatively normal bedtime mishap was presumably a consequence of the stress and anxiety caused by my parents' divorce. However, my bed-wetting continued to an age far beyond the realms of normality. So regularly did this night-time routine play out and so severe was the problem that medical advice, both psychological and physiological, was sought to establish how to cure this particular problem.

Although the issue was relatively severe at the time, I eventually grew out of it, and not since I was a rather confused and very emotional eleven-year-old had I wet the bed. Patrick changed all that too.

The first time it happened during Patrick's stay, I woke up in the middle of the night and was genuinely confused about what could possibly have happened to have caused my bed sheets to be in such a condition. I had experienced night sweats prior to my diagnosis, and continued to have them periodically during my treatment, but this felt different. I considered the possibility of having spilt a drink, even though I never take a drink to bed. Perhaps one of the children had spilt something? It wasn't any of those things. Only one possible answer remained. I had wet the bed.

The feelings of embarrassment, shame and confusion that I felt as a child when I had to confess to my mum that I had wet the bed came flooding back. Thankfully, this time, there was no one with me to whom I had to confess. I cannot even begin to imagine how it would have felt having to disclose to my partner I had wet the bed. The crushing embarrassment of such a revelation would then have been compounded by the fact that my broken body would have had to sit by while she removed and changed all the bed linen. At that point my humiliation would have been well and truly complete.

However, the joy of knowing that I had preserved a minuscule piece of dignity was balanced against the realisation that the responsibility for the clean-up fell to me. How was I going to change the bed? I couldn't put my socks on without getting out of breath. How on earth was I going to strip a bed and put on a new fitted sheet and duvet cover? It would take all the energy I had just to get them out of the cupboard, never mind put them on.

The answer was simple. Skin-crawlingly embarrassing, somewhat disgusting, but simple. I didn't. I couldn't. Instead I simply slept on the other side of the bed until the days in my two-weekly cycle when I was strong enough to do it. Just another day devoid of dignity. These were the levels of loathsomeness I had sunk to.

Thank you, Patrick.

DUVET DAYS & BINGE EATING

So pathetic was I for much of my time with Patrick that the simplest of activities became impossible, and everyday chores developed into something so disproportionately difficult that they were almost unmanageable.

Even something as simple as climbing the stairs became problematic. I would frequently have to stop for a break whilst trying. If my failed Herculean efforts to get me to bed coincided with one of Patrick's less spiteful days, he would offer assistance. But Patrick's unique brand of encouragement was akin to that of a physical training instructor in the army 'encouraging' new recruits around an obstacle course or on a 10km TAB. He would bark words of inspiration in my ear, intended to persuade me to discover previously unattainable levels of physical fortitude: 'Get up the stairs, Fry, you ridiculous waste of space' or 'You're pathetic, Fry, it's a flight of stairs, it's not fucking Mount Everest!' On other occasions he resorted to more psychological forms of motivation.

He would whisper in my ear, 'What would your children think if they could see you right now? Who wants a Daddy who can't even get himself upstairs to bed?' As was so often the case, Patrick had become the mouthpiece for my own very real thoughts and feelings.

If my struggles coincided with one of his days off from his role of professional motivational shitbag, he would attempt to offer a degree of physical help. This support amounted to attempting to pull me up by the hand or standing behind me and trying to push. Neither ever worked, as my little companion was nowhere near strong enough to shift this dead weight up the stairs. He soon abandoned his rather forlorn attempts at non-verbal assistance and resorted to his previous brand of 'motivation' instead. He definitely enjoyed that far more.

As my treatment progressed, getting upstairs became so much of an issue that I got into a routine of knowing that, on certain days, come bedtime, the prospect of having to climb the stairs would be so utterly demoralising and, quite frankly, a pain in the arse, I would neither want nor have even the slightest inclination to bother. I habitually pre-empted that feeling by bringing the duvet and pillows down with me in the morning and sleeping on the sofa that night, and the next few nights.

Camping out on the sofa on my own very unique kind of Duvet Day did not offer any greater chance of an adequate night's sleep, but, with a loo downstairs, it did at least mean that negotiating the stairs was one less thing for me to think about.

On more than one occasion Patrick suggested a

potential solution to this particular dilemma, the basis for which I was never able to establish.

'Why don't you set up a tent and camp in the garden?'

'What!? You must be kidding!?'

'Actually, I'm very serious.' He seemed almost upset that I would question the sincerity of his suggestion. 'The weather's lovely and you might find it easier to sleep in the slightly cooler air.'

My inability to sleep because of the discomfort I had been experiencing certainly wasn't being helped by the warm night-time temperatures. Perhaps camping in the garden would help. But hang on.

'Why are you being nice? What's the catch?'

'No catch. I was just trying to help, but if you don't want my help…' He waved his paw indifferently and wandered off.

I very quickly dismissed Patrick's suggestion, not because of my intrinsic suspicion of his motives, but because of my evolutionary objection to sleeping outside.

I continued to sleep downstairs, and not in the garden, on my bad days, but never when the children were with me. I didn't want them to have to think about why Daddy was sleeping on the sofa. After all, I couldn't explain it away by telling them that I had pissed off their mother and was in the doghouse, or had been snoring so loudly that I had been dismissed from the marital bed and banished to the sofa. I wanted things to stay as 'normal' as possible for them.

Not every day was a torrent of discomfort and difficulty, however. Patrick and I had days when things weren't completely hideous. We were, on occasion, able to spend some time together in a perfectly relaxed and non-confrontational way. I could relax and drink tea from my 'Patrick is a C@*t' mug. Tea that I had made without exhausting myself, and that I could actually taste. I could consume copious amounts of crap food and do anything else I wanted, as long as the chosen activity didn't involve me getting off my arse. Inertia remained very much my state of choice/necessity.

Patrick and I would often just sit and read, listen to music or watch the cricket. He was not a great fan of the game, though, and was most definitely not au fait with its etiquette, tactics and many nuances. His constant interjections and queries about the rules and what was going on often drove me to distraction, but I always remained very calm and considered in my responses, acutely aware of how quickly his mood could change. I never wanted to rile him and awaken the beast, who would then see to it that my relatively calm and relaxing day rapidly turned into something very different.

Patrick loved to talk. He was always wittering on about something or other. Everywhere I went, everything I did, Patrick was there, chatting away. In many ways he was quite a jolly companion. Very little seemed to get him down and he was almost exclusively positive about the topics he wanted to discuss. However, most of his chosen subject matter related to my treatment and its consequences. This was where our perspectives diverged significantly. He took a disturbingly high degree of pleasure from seeing me suffer in any way. He got a rush from observing my struggles with the physical and mental angst he had caused. He liked nothing more than to sit beside me and provide a commentary on every aspect of our lives together.

The school run ceased to be a routine for just the four of us. Patrick would often escort me and the Small Frys on our drive to school. He would position himself in the vacant seat in the back of the car and chat away, almost incessantly, throughout the ten or so minutes our journey took. Adding his voice to the cacophony of noise that always accompanied our daily outings was maddening. Any parent of more than one child will tell you how exasperating it can be to have several voices all talking to you simultaneously, each seeking, if not demanding, your full, undivided attention. Adding Patrick to the mix of Mollie, Libby and Will, all talking to me at the same time, made my head spin. Appeals for a bit of peace and quiet had to be made non-personal for fear of inadvertently shouting, 'Patrick, will you please shut the fuck up!' This would have been wrong and somewhat counter-productive on several levels. As well as engendering the perfectly reasonable question, 'Daddy, who's Patrick?' from one or all of my children, it would also have created a number of other issues.

First, I have always tried to avoid shouting at my children. A raised voice, a change of tone, yes. Shouting, not if I can help it. Having said that I am not a saint, and have a relatively low patience threshold, so I would be lying if I was to claim that the façade of parental perfection had not slipped from time to time.

Second, whilst I am not averse to cursing – I actually enjoy the use of a bit of 'choice' language – I've always tried, particularly when they were younger, to avoid the use of profanities in my children's presence.

Third, and probably most important, I had no desire to make my children aware of either the imaginary companion that was joining us on our journey to school, or of the fact that their father was not only hearing voices, but was willing to enter into discussions with the buddy in his head. It's been a while since I read any guide to good parenting, but I'm guessing that 'Do not freak your children out or permanently scar them mentally by chatting openly with make-believe characters who exist only in your imagination' must be quite high up the list of Don'ts.

Primary school teachers are frequently fed information about the parents of the children in their class by the pupils themselves. Although most of it is dismissed with a smile and a reassuring 'Thank you for sharing that with me', some comments live rather longer in the memory. Some will make the teacher see the parent(s) in a completely different light and make parents' evening rather more fun, whilst the best ones are saved, noted and shared in the staffroom.

For instance: 'My mummy has two different personalities: one at home and one in front of grandma' or 'My mummy drank two bottles of wine last night.' Or:

Teacher: Can you tell me something that has a key?
Child 1: Handcuffs.
Child 2: My mummy has some of those.
(Child 2's mummy is not a police officer.)

I am sure having one of my children go into school and tell their teacher and classmates, 'My daddy has a friend that he talks to but who we can't see' may have caused some alarm and no little hilarity amongst the staff at breaktime.

Towards the end of my two-week cycle, I would have a couple of clear days when Patrick wasn't around and I felt as close to my pre-chemo self as I ever did during those seven months. There were days – days a friend of mine described as 'flopping days' – when I was able to relax and do nothing, relatively free from discomfort. I lived with a permanent underlying sense of nausea, the metallic taste in my mouth and heartburn; but, on good days, these were bearable when compared with the feelings I faced for the majority of the fortnightly routine. In addition to 'flopping' and enjoying the relative freedom of it all, these days were spent focusing on achieving two primary objectives: chores and eating.

All the household jobs that I was unable to do during my shittier days had to be done in that forty-eight-hour window. It often felt like some strange game show in which I had to get as much as possible done in a prescribed time to be successful. I'm not sure I would ever tout it to a television production company, though. It wouldn't have been a great viewing spectacle and the prizes were crap.

The chores were all very normal and mundane, but because of the time pressures involved they took on an increased significance. I had to get the washing, cleaning, tidying up and shopping done. I became a domestic god on acid. If I was successful and met my objectives, by the time I'd finished, and the clothes were clean and the cupboards were fully stocked, the house resembled an IKEA showroom. That didn't often happen. Although I did feel much better during those two days, the weeks and months of inertia soon caught up with me. I very quickly found myself running on empty and unable to complete my tasks. Yet another failure.

On more than one occasion I either didn't get myself sufficiently organised or ran out of the requisite amount of energy on my 'good days' to buy everything I needed for the children. This meant an outing with Patrick to Tesco on one of my shittier days.

Patrick always loved these trips. It was an ideal opportunity for him to once again make life as difficult as he possibly could for me. Like some feral toddler he would hang off the trolley, climb in and out incessantly, generally get in the way and throw in items that I didn't want while I wasn't looking. Pushing the trolley along what seemed like never-ending aisles with my uncontrollable assistant often became too much physically. When it did, and my body would not allow me to stand any longer, I made my way, with my trolley, to the seats at the front of the store so I could sit down in an attempt to summon up enough strength to continue my mission. The huge sense of relief at being able to stop and take the weight off my aching legs and feet, and rest my broken body, was tempered by the knowledge that I would eventually have to get up again and resume my shopping, unless I intended to simply sit there for the rest of the day.

My fellow shoppers walked past me wheeling trolleys full of their newly purchased goodies, having successfully completed the most routine of activities. Routine it may have been for them, but for me it was a routine that, once again, had proved too much, my pathetic-ness having rocketed to new levels.

Stuck, almost literally, in those seats, part of me wanted to address the embarrassment I was feeling. The other shoppers often flicked a look of confusion and scepticism my way as they passed. Why is that bloke just sitting there? That's not normal behaviour… They were right, it wasn't normal behaviour. By way of an explanation, I wanted to announce: 'I've got cancer, and I'm having chemotherapy, which means that my body is so bloody useless I can't even buy a few groceries to feed my children without feeling like I've just run a marathon, uphill, at altitude, with Patrick on my back, and then been hit by a truck as I crossed the finish line.'

I was frustrated that they didn't already know that. Why didn't they know? Surely it was obvious? Clearly it wasn't. I felt as though I should be wearing a sign around my neck like some modern-day leper. Once again, the embarrassment and frustration I felt at not being able to perform the most basic and fundamental of chores reared their ugly heads.

Throughout these sorry episodes Patrick sat in the trolley smugly, contentedly munching his way through a bar of chocolate that I had neither said he could have nor paid for. Shopping with my three children in tow had always been a challenge. However, shopping with Patrick made me long for those days. I would have given anything to have got rid of Patrick and had the Small Frys back with me. I missed their incessant requests for this, that and the other, running off, squabbling about who was going to sit in the trolley; my constant demands to 'Put that back', 'Don't touch that', 'Sit down in the trolley', and the often unsuccessful attempts to avoid any escapes. 'Where the hell has Libby gone now?' was a frequently repeated refrain in our local supermarket. Having shopped with Patrick, this all now seemed like a retail utopia.

As well as getting everything I needed for the children, shopping expeditions were primarily concerned with stocking up on the piles of crap I would need to fuel the eating binges that were the other objective of that two-day period.

Eating became a priority during that time because I knew I had forty-eight hours when my mouth was less uncomfortable, and I could actually taste what I was eating. This inevitably resulted in me embarking on what can only be described as a crisp-, biscuit- and chocolate-fuelled binge. I was like a demented snacker who had been sponsored to eat as much crap as was humanly possible in two days. It was glorious. A calorie-filled, sugar-coated, biscuit-wrapped indulgence. I loved my binge days. I looked forward to them. I don't know if it was the satisfaction that they induced or the major sugar rush that followed my overindulgence, but whatever it was, even Patrick became a peripheral figure in my consciousness during these snacking orgies. They made me really happy.

NOT A GREAT TIME TO BE SINGLE

For the first time since I was fourteen, I found myself properly single. This, I soon realised, was not a great time to not have someone permanent in my life. To be without any support when you are told that you are about to enter a period when you will need more support than you have ever done before is far from ideal. I had, immediately prior to my cancer day and at least for a while afterwards, 'friends with benefits', so I was not without people to spend time with.

These 'relationships' soon petered out once the effects of my treatment took hold. Chemotherapy and its many side effects are not attractive.

There were many times when I desperately needed someone to help me. Someone to look after me, support me, provide and care for me when I was feeling rough – very rough; someone to provide support through all the utter hideousness, pain and discomfort; someone to be my body when I couldn't move, my mind when I couldn't think, and the resurrector of identity when mine was completely lost.

Dealing with the cancer and the treatment was tough. Of course, I had Patrick with me, but living with him was the equivalent of cohabiting with a drunk, unemployed, chain smoking couch potato – completely bloody useless. In fact, he just made things worse. Trying to get through all the crap he threw at me alone was incredibly difficult. Add to the mix looking after three relatively small children and running a house and I was suddenly faced with what appeared to be an impossible task. However, that was how it was going to be, and it was a task I would simply have to get on with.

Having cancer, and the course of treatment I embarked on with just Patrick to accompany me, was a very insular experience. The only people close enough to me to be affected were my children and they were too young to appreciate exactly what was happening other than knowing that Daddy wasn't very well.

I went through all my appointments, chemo sessions, scans and home visits alone. I was solely responsible for ensuring I took all my medication, for preparing all my own meals, doing my own washing and household chores, all of which frequently didn't happen, doing the school run and looking after and caring for my children. My lack of ability to do anything other than that which absolutely had to be done meant that the basics frequently fell apart and the children and I effectively missed out on six months together, a whole summer and autumn.

Not having someone to talk to about and share the process and my journey with Patrick, other than Patrick, was often difficult. However, it was in some ways, and certainly in hindsight, not such a bad thing.

Although there were times when the sense of loneliness and helplessness was overwhelming, being alone freed me from any sense of obligation I am certain I would have felt if there had been someone around. I would have found the requirement to remain 'positive' and to put a brave face on things in order to not upset or unduly concern those closest to me a crushing burden. Supporting a loved one through cancer must be incredibly difficult, stressful and upsetting. I think I would have found the pressure of trying not to add to that stress and upset them further far too hard. Being on my own meant I didn't have to pretend to anyone except my children. I could have my bad days, days when I didn't want to or couldn't do anything, without worrying about how that might impact on someone else. I was free to feel miserable and, on occasion, to feel sorry for myself. I was allowed to be angry when I wanted to.

I was able to derive pleasure from some of the simplest things. My binge days were a particular highlight of my time with Patrick. Although he prevented me from eating at all for most of my bi-weekly treatment cycles, on his days off I was allowed whatever I wanted, and I most definitely made the most of it. It was like being a kid when your parents are out and you have access to all the goodies in the house.

If there had been someone close to me, someone looking after me, they would, almost certainly, have prevented me from indulging in this way, insisting instead that I eat healthily during those periods in order to aid my treatment. I am fairly certain I would have killed anyone, however well intentioned, who tried to take away that packet of chocolate digestives (it was very common for me to eat a whole packet in one sitting), family size bag of Sensations crisps (a whole bag was often my dinner), and the sharing bag of M&Ms or giant bar of Dairy Milk. Going through chemotherapy provides very few opportunities for genuine pleasure. Being able to indulge in that way was a pleasure unlike almost any other I have ever experienced. I am rather glad I didn't have someone around to take that away from me.

Aware of my lack of partner to discuss my concerns, anxieties and fears with, Patrick would often try to fill that void.

'You know you can always talk to me. Tell me how you're feeling. It might help to offload.'

Whilst this offer to assist sounded sincere enough, it was odd in the extreme that such a proposition of assistance should come from the very source of my misery. In fact, it was all rather too odd. So, as much as I really needed to have someone to offload to, Patrick's suggestion was merely an attempt to exploit my vulnerabilities. I refused to be duped by him. It was a carefully contrived fishing expedition to gather evidence about his endeavours to date and information as to those aspects of his treatment of me that I was finding most difficult.

I never took Patrick up on his offer. I had no desire to become a foundation for his research and a conduit to him becoming even better at what he does. In addition to my reluctance to assist Patrick in any way in his repugnant little project, I do not subscribe to the notion that a 'problem shared is a problem halved'. In reality, simply telling someone else about any issue you are struggling with does nothing to solve the conundrum. A problem shared is just a problem someone else knows about. On this basis, and the fact that I didn't trust him any further than I could throw him, and although Patrick and I would spend an indecent amount of time together, he would never become my confidant.

THAT'S NOT COURAGE

Cancer sufferers, most often those whose residence on their own Isle of Patrick became a permanent one, are frequently described as having faced their illness and treatment with 'courage' or are reported as having been 'brave' in the face of their struggles with cancer.

People die every day from illnesses they may have had and grappled with for months or even years – dementia, heart disease, liver failure, motor neurone disease – but rarely are they described as having been 'brave' or commended for having faced their condition in the same spirited way that cancer sufferers are. I do not understand why that is.

I have a pink wristband I bought to help raise money for breast cancer research. Inscribed on it are the words 'hope, faith, strength, courage', signifying the characteristics needed by anyone who faces their own 'battle' with cancer.

I agree wholeheartedly that anyone with cancer will indeed need hope, for without hope all the hideousness would quite simply too much to bear. Faith is not necessarily needed in a religious sense, but faith in something helps. And strength – both mental and physical – is required in bucket loads if we are to complete the journey in a positive way. But courage? No.

Dealing with cancer, the treatments and all the crap that comes with it, and the very real prospect that you may not survive, is a struggle of terrifying proportions. Living through and surviving such a struggle is one of the most difficult things I have had to do, but the fact that getting through it is incredibly hard is not the same as courage.

I do not see anything about what I did on my journey with Patrick as being brave or courageous. I had a little fucker of a companion and his groups of miscreant cells that wanted to kill me. I didn't want them to, but there was basically nothing I could do about it. I put all my faith in the medical professionals who cared for me during Patrick's stay. My view was, if Patrick didn't kill me, it would be because the drugs with which these marvellous people had poisoned my system for six hideous months had done their job. Getting through that process had nothing to do with courage on my part.

I didn't want to die, simple as that. I didn't want to die because I wanted my children to grow up with me being there for them, but that is not an entirely selfless aspiration, because I wanted that for me too. I wanted to see them grow up. I wanted to watch them develop into the children, young people and adults they are going to be. I didn't want to die because I had things I still wanted to do with my life. I was nowhere near ready to stop.

I endured the treatment and all the vileness, pain and discomfort that came with it because I wanted to get through it. I wanted to finish my journey. I wanted to play a full ninety minutes. I did not want to be substituted. That's not bravery or courage, it's self-preservation.

Members of the armed forces putting their lives on the line in a war zone, police officers confronting street protestors during a riot, activists around the world vigorously fighting oppressive governments in their pursuit of democracy, members of the public tackling wannabe suicide bombers, frontline NHS staff continuing to treat patients during the coronavirus pandemic – that's bravery, that's courage. Simply not wanting to die is not; it is one of the most natural instincts we all have and the epitome of self-interest.

BYE, DAD

'Ian, you need to come to see your dad today.'

It was 9:00am on a Saturday morning in January and my stepmother was ringing to update me on the situation regarding my terminally ill father.

'The MacMillan nurses have been to see him this morning and they've said it's likely he won't survive the day.'

In other words, if I wanted to see him again before he died, it was today or not at all. That decision was rather more difficult than I would have previously imagined. Of course, I wanted the opportunity to say goodbye to my dad. He was my idol – albeit a severely flawed idol – but I had to consider whether I would rather remember him as he was or as the frail, skeletal, shadow of the man I loved but who could hardly breathe let alone actually communicate with me.

Having juggled mentally with that question for the best part of the day, it wasn't until 4:30pm that afternoon that I decided I did want to say goodbye. As I drove the twenty minutes to his house, I was fraught with worry that I had left my decision too late. What if I got there and he had already died? Would he die believing that his eldest child and only son had not made the effort to come and see him? How would I feel if I had denied us the chance to say that final goodbye?

I arrived at the house. My sisters and stepmother were in the lounge. I raced up the stairs to his bedroom, discarding my jacket behind me as I went. His neighbour was sitting on a chair next to the bed where my dad lay. As I burst into the room, she smiled and, without saying a word, left.

I sat on the bed beside him. He was a withered caricature of himself, barely recognisable as the man I adored. It was heart-breaking to see him in such a terrible state. His cancer had devastated his entire being. He was breathing only fitfully and often gasping for air. The sounds coming out of his destroyed body were incredibly upsetting.

I held his hand and spoke to him to let him know I was there. I remember reading somewhere that it is widely believed that the final sense to fail in the dying is hearing. His other senses had certainly departed. I was therefore hoping that what I had read was right.

I talked to him about my memories of him and our relationship. The memories were not as extensive as one would normally expect of a thirty-two-year-old and his father, however. After my parents' divorce, for the remainder of my childhood, I had seen my dad for only a few hours every Saturday. I didn't therefore have many of the memories that a man of my age might have of his dad – playing football in the garden, doing DIY, cleaning the car, family holidays, or going to sporting events together. There were some memories nevertheless, and they were good memories.

One thing that I had always hoped and strived for was to make him proud. It was not a question I had ever asked of him before, so I took this last opportunity to ask. Why, I'm not sure, because I knew it was now too late to ever get an answer to that question.

As I savoured every second of being with him for the last time, I remember feeling contrasting emotions as to my role in this relationship. Holding my father's hand made me feel like a child, although I have no recollection of my dad ever holding my hand or showing any physical emotion towards me. Nevertheless, part of me regressed into childhood, my dad holding my hand.

At the same time the situation felt very much like a role reversal, with me, a much physically bigger man, as the adult and my dying dad as the weak, poorly child who needed my support and reassurance. It was a role I was utterly unprepared for. It felt unnatural and wrong to be playing the part of the adult in our relationship. I didn't like it. I wanted to be the child again.

I felt cheated. My dad was too young to die. We had spent so little time together, and there was still so much I wanted to do as adult father and son. Why hadn't I used some of the time we'd had as adults to do some of the things I wanted to do – go to the pub together, watch sport, or just sit and put the world to rights? All these opportunities were about to be taken away from me for good and I had missed them. My dad was literally dying in front of me.

I spent the time we had trying to eke out every

remaining ounce from what remained of my relationship with my old man. I desperately tried to think of all the things I wanted to say to him before he was gone forever. Why, I asked myself, hadn't I given this any thought before now? I had long known my dad was dying. Why hadn't I been better prepared?

Ten short minutes after I had arrived my dad took his last very audible breath and was gone. For half an hour I just sat there with him while we waited for the undertaker to come and take his body away. I held his hand, not wanting to let go. It was just me and him together, in silence. I suddenly became acutely aware that this would be the last time I would see him. I didn't want to say goodbye and for that to be the end of our relationship. Despite how difficult it was sitting there with him during his last few minutes, it felt right that it was me who was with him as he died.

Although he never gave any indication that he even knew I was there, I still tell myself that he waited until he had seen me before being overcome by this evil disease. I do however accept that the timing may simply have been coincidental and my somewhat egotistical view of my dad holding out in order to await the arrival of his prodigal son may have been a complete nonsense that I told myself to feel better about the fact that I didn't get my arse over to see him earlier.

Before Patrick turned up, my dad's tortuous demise was my only real close-up experience of cancer and what it can do to a person. My dad's journey with cancer had ended in a spectacularly devastating way. I was now faced with the fact that I was on a similar journey. I could only hope that mine ended rather better for me and my children than it had for my dad and his.

SURVIVOR GUILT

I had never met Mr C before his wife approached me in the Sunshine Room while I was tethered to my machine, and he to his, and introduced us across the room.

We never had the opportunity to meet again. I did, however, teach both his boys.

I bumped into Mrs I one day after dropping the children off at school. Her eldest daughter had been in my very first class at the school I was teaching at when Patrick arrived, and I therefore knew her a little better.

She too was in the midst of chemotherapy.

She was a woman of unerring religious faith and was remarkably positive about the whole thing, utterly convinced that her faith would ensure a successful completion to her journey.

She was also a strong advocate of the effectiveness of alternative remedies.

A couple of days after our meeting I received a card from her.

It read:

'Dear Ian

You have been so much in my thoughts and prayers these recent months as we have both been dealing with chemo and cancer…I think of you often and hold you in my prayers. Chemo is horrid and I can't imagine how you find the strength to do it on your own. I hope you do not feel that you are utterly alone because there are so many people rooting for you, me amongst them.

I don't know if you would find it helpful or not but if you are interested there is a man who knows a great deal about keeping people well from cancer who has been helping me with complimentary diet, techniques, etc. … He is not a doctor … I have found him <u>really</u> helpful. I have a feeling he may be very helpful to you.

All the best'

The sentiment and the feeling in this letter still has a real effect on me. The love with which the letter was sent is evident and was very gratefully received. However, my gratitude is tinged with a very real sense of anger. Anger that such a kind and genuine woman could be duped into believing that the destination of her journey with cancer would be decided by anything other than drugs and luck. I have no issue with anyone taking solace in a faith or a higher spiritual being if it helps them to get through the daily hideousness that is chemotherapy. What frustrates me is that genuine, trusting, forgiving people can be led to believe that surviving their journey is dependent upon or controlled by anything other than medicine and good fortune.

Mr C and Mrs I both died shortly after I had completed my treatment. Both these deaths were a tragedy, in the very truest sense of that much-overused word. Both had a spouse and a young family. I have absolutely no idea how their children, particularly, coped with such a loss. To lose a parent at such a young age is unimaginably cruel and put my feelings about losing my dad when I was thirty-two into perspective.

Both had so much to live for, as did I, but luck dictated that of the three of us only I would survive my time with Patrick. That is all it is. Luck. I am no more deserving than either of them to go on living my life with my children, experiencing the things I will experience and seeing the places I will see before I am finally substituted off. When I think about Mr C and Mrs I, which I do, frequently, I have two overriding emotions. Guilt and unfairness.

I feel a tangible guilt that I am still here living and enjoying my life for no other reason than my drugs worked and theirs didn't. Guilt because I continue to be able to nurture, observe and enjoy my children and they don't.

Despite what anyone may tell us about the ways in which we can prevent, cure or overcome our cancers, the reality of it is that the whole thing is completely arbitrary. Just as the chance of getting cancer in the first place is simply a matter of luck – although there are a number of self-induced factors that increase the risk – no faith, diet or homeopathic treatment guarantees a successful end to the journey. It is a lottery. A roll of a dice. A toss of a coin. There is no rhyme nor reason to it. It is nothing but luck that means my children still have me, whilst Mr C's and Mrs I's children will grow up without them. It is not fair.

I remember bumping into Mrs C outside the school gates one afternoon shortly after her husband had died.

We just stood and looked at each other for a moment. I was, unusually, utterly lost for words. We hugged. This was no token hug. There was nothing superficial about it. I held her in a way I have never held anyone before or since. It was a wordless exchange between two people, who despite hardly knowing each other had a most unwanted bond. A connection that is impossible to explain.

As we released each other I felt compelled to say something. To address the elephant in the playground, i.e., the fact that I was here and her husband wasn't. My children still had both their parents and hers didn't. I looked her in the eye and said, 'I'm so sorry. It isn't fair.' She agreed. My expression of regret was not just for her loss. It was also an apology for the fact that I was still alive.

It was unfair because her children no longer had their father, but mine did. Unfair because I get, in the assumed way all parents are guilty of, to continue to see my children grow. To see them develop into young adults and make their own way in the world. Unfair because I get to spend time with my children exploring new places, doing new things and continue doing the things we/they particularly enjoy again and again. Unfair because I can create long-lasting memories for both me and them. Unfair because I will get to counsel and advise my children in a way that only a father can.

In the time since I completed my treatment, I have already taken my children on their inaugural plane flight to their first holiday abroad and to their first live football and rugby matches. I've helped Mollie prepare for high school and advised her on her GCSE options (although she didn't listen!). I've dealt with issues the children were having at school. I have watched Libby and Will make their acting debuts with a local drama group, and stood on the touch line as they represented their school for the first time on the sports field. I've watched Libby add to an ever-growing collection of gymnastics medals and proudly attended parents' evenings, class assemblies and dance workshops for all three of them. I have taken Mollie to her first theatre production and Libby to the ballet.

I have accompanied Will on the start of his football journey, albeit a journey he started rather late, having spent his first nine years declaring an absolute lack of interest in the sport. Whilst I am delighted that we now have this additional shared interest, his choice of team to support did cause me considerable angst. Can there be any greater evidence of a father's unconditional love for his son than not having him adopted when he declares himself a Manchester United fan?

As a family we have ridden bikes, played in the garden, walked up and rolled down the Malvern Hills, visited our capital city to explore the wonders of my and the girls' hometown, been on holidays and enjoyed numerous adventures and experiences.

Like all dads, I have developed a growing, unpaid side-line as 'Daddy's Taxi', ferrying my increasingly active children all over the county to sporting, drama and social events. They undoubtedly have a more active social life than I do.

Their growing use of this provision, along with the continued daily school run service, does at least provide me with the opportunity to indulge in one of the most important Daddy-specific roles: expanding their musical education by making them listen to my music in the car.

There is also a more serious side to Daddy duties. With Mollie now venturing out alone with her friends, I have become 'Paranoid Dad'. Even more important, and the duty I take most seriously of all, for duty it most certainly is, is my obligation to be 'Embarrassing Dad', a responsibility most lovingly performed in public and as frequently as possible.

Mr C, and his boys, had all that taken away from them.

I saw the boys every day at school. That was really hard. I wanted so much to be able to help them, but it felt like offering any kind of help would be tantamount to rubbing salt into their unhealable wounds. Every day I thought about what they were going through and how the fears that my children had expressed about me dying had become a reality for them.

The guilt I felt and continue to feel, not just in relation to Mr C and Mrs I, but all those who don't successfully complete their journey and who become another of Patrick's victims, is the strangest of feelings. The most genuine and overwhelming sadness I feel for those who did not survive, and for the associated pain and suffering of their loved ones, is coupled with the obvious selfish joy that, by sheer good fortune, I managed to avoid the same fate. They are emotions that are extremely difficult to reconcile in my head.

To some, 'survivor guilt' may seem a rather shallow, meaningless and self-pitying emotion. In many ways they are probably right. I certainly have those feelings about it. Patrick most certainly had very little time for the idea of survivor guilt.

'Not this again! You're still here. Get over it. Their Patrick just had rather more success with them than I'm having with you!'

Nevertheless, the feelings of guilt are very real. I am not able to get my head around the fact that I am still here and so many others, some of whom I knew, are not.

SOMEWHERE BETWEEN SHIT AND SYPHILIS

'If you're looking for sympathy, you'll find it in the dictionary somewhere between shit and syphilis.'

This was Patrick's rather ruthless, dismissive and oft repeated assessment of any perceived notion of me feeling sorry for myself at any point during our time together. On those days when the whole thing got a little too much for me, I could rest easy in the knowledge that Patrick would ensure I never lost sight of the reality of my situation, particularly in relation to those thousands of others whose suffering was far greater than mine.

'I don't understand you sometimes. Have you lost all sense of perspective, Fry? You do know things could be so much worse? You're still alive – at least for the time being.' The obvious joy with which Patrick added the time caveat to that statement not only prompted his desired shift in perspective, it also reminded me of what a little shit Patrick really was.

Patrick's reality checks were occasionally brutal, always honest, and, as much as it pains me to admit, accurate. Throughout my treatment and whilst writing this book I always attempted to avoid indulging in too much self-pitying. There were, I think, naturally, many occasions when I felt more than a little sorry for myself, but I remained, for most of my time with Patrick, true to my very pragmatic self about the whole thing. Either Patrick kills me, or he doesn't. It is what it is. It was remarkably straightforward really.

Despite all the wonders I experienced while resident on the Isle of Patrick, I was, I am and I will always be acutely aware of the fact that there were, are and will be those on their own journey, whose adventures will be far worse, more painful, more distressing and more terrifying than mine. There have and will always be those who suffer more as a result of their treatment, and far too many who will not complete their journey at all. I know a number of people who fit into these categories.

This kind of personal knowledge is extremely sobering and acts as a constant reminder of just how much worse my experiences could have been. I owe it to those whose reconstructed bodies act as a permanent reminder of their own extensive suffering, and to the memory of those whose journey ended in the most definitive way possible, to never overestimate or exaggerate my own difficulties and to ensure I remain firmly rooted in a contextual reality and acknowledge my place in a cancer-induced scale of suffering. Patrick really helped with that, although not always in as sympathetic a way as I would have liked.

I have never diverged from the acknowledgement of the often-unimaginable suffering of others. However, comparisons are not always terribly helpful. Being regularly reminded, either by myself, Patrick or others, of my own relatively lowly status in the cancer suffering hierarchy was, on occasion, enormously disheartening and engendered feelings of shame, embarrassment and guilt that I was even considering feeling sorry for myself.

Suffering should not be a commodity assessed as a relative statement. Regardless of whether your glass is half empty, half full, completely dry or overflowing, it is okay to occasionally feel the need to pick the bloody thing up and throw it against the wall. We can only live our own lives, experience our own experiences and travel on our own journey. We should not be made to feel guilty about feeling and declaring our pain, expressing our concerns about where our journey ends, or having those days when we acknowledge to ourselves and those around us that our travels are frequently overwhelming and indulging in a little bit of self-pity. Our pain, emotions, anxieties and fears are real. The fact that there are, and there will always be, many whose suffering is greater does not make our own suffering or fears less valid.

NO MORE SUNSHINE ROOM

I had long identified Wednesday 20th November as my target date. Another hugely significant day in my life with Patrick. A milestone in our journey. The date beyond which nothing else really mattered.

It was one of those events that in normal circumstances would have merited a physical record of such a momentous occasion. Perhaps a selfie of me and my companion to record this crossroads in proceedings, in the same way that you might take a picture with a partner to celebrate your anniversary, or at a long-wished-for venue in your travels together.

This was my final scheduled chemotherapy session.

Like all the other noteworthy events and experiences associated with my adventures with Patrick, I felt it should have merited a demonstrable reaction. My last chemotherapy session should, I thought, be a cause for celebration, but that wasn't how it felt. I was certainly delighted to be leaving the Sunshine Room for what, I hoped beyond hope, would be the last time.

Never again would I have to spend those long, long Wednesdays sat in my chair, plugged into a machine dispensing poison into my system, the constant pinging of machines reverberating around the room like an unstoppable alarm clock, and unable to escape Patrick's constant whinging and mischief making.

I wanted to feel ecstatic about completing stage one of my liberation from Patrick's occupation thanks to the efforts of the army of staff and drugs lead by Major General Dr Fiona Clark. When the time came, far from feeling euphoric, I actually found it hard, no matter how much I wanted to feel differently, to become too excited and self-congratulating. In no way did it feel like an 'accomplishment' to have got to this stage. In reality, I had done nothing. My only job in the whole process was to turn up for each of my sessions and sit for long enough for the drugs to be delivered. Not much of an achievement. Dr Clark had led me through stage one, but the next stage was down to me.

Undoubtedly, one of the other reasons for my lack of enthusiasm about having completed twelve sessions and six months of chemotherapy was I knew there was every chance that this was by no means the end. In fact, it could well be simply the beginning of the very end.

In order to establish how successful, or not, six months of poisoning me had been, Dr Clark sent me for a scan to establish whether Patrick and his little bastard cells were sticking around for more fun and frolics at my expense. This next stage of the process would give us a definitive answer as to whether or not the treatment had been a success and had had the desired effect on the little fucker that had dominated my life for the preceding seven months.

If the treatment had been successful, I would go into remission, a post chemotherapy state. The holy grail of cancer treatment. The ultimate prize: Patrick's gone and you are free to leave his island.

NO COMPASSION

Having worked as much as was physically possible for the three weeks that remained of the summer term following my first chemo session, it was agreed, on the advice of Dr Clark, that I would remain absent from school for the whole of the autumn term, i.e. from September to the beginning of the Christmas holiday in early December, and thereafter I would be guided by Dr Clark as to when I should, assuming the treatment was successful, return to work.

This agreement not only provided me with the freedom to undertake my treatment without the worry and pressure of having to return to school during that time, it was also a better option for the children in my class. The uncertainty of not knowing whether I would be in school, depending on whether I was having a shit or less shit day, would not have been good for them. Making that decision enabled the school to bring in a replacement teacher who could provide the children with some continuity.

Nevertheless, despite my absence I kept in regular

contact with school, keeping them abreast of my treatment, dates and general progress. I provided assistance where I could, including attending parents' evening meetings and writing reports at the end of the summer term. I was also regularly at school in my capacity as a parent, delivering and collecting my children at the beginning and end of the day.

Just a few days after my final chemotherapy session I was contacted by my headteacher and asked to attend a meeting at school. I assumed we were just going to have a catch up and discuss how we could take matters forward with regard to my eventual return to work.

The school had already finished for the Christmas break so there were no children or teachers around when I arrived. It was an environment in which I felt extremely comfortable and very much at home. I always liked being in school during the holidays. I had absolutely no feelings of apprehension about the meeting, given what I thought our discussion was to be about. That sense of ease was very quickly dispelled.

The meeting was initially concerned with what I thought at the time were genuine enquiries about my health and discussing possible dates for my return to work. Dr Clark had recommended I remain off work until after the Easter holidays and thereafter to have a phased return. She had always said that, generally speaking, the length of time it takes a patient to recover from intensive chemotherapy is equivalent to how long they have chemotherapy for, so, in my case, six months. On that basis I would not be fully recovered until around June. We were only in December.

Having begun in a pleasant enough way, the meeting took an unexpected turn, one that was to have enormous ramifications for me, my life and those of my children. A senior non-teaching member of the school's leadership team, whose presence at the meeting had puzzled me from the outset, explained that 'in accordance with school policy' I had been placed on half pay with effect from the beginning of that month, some ten days earlier, having reached the school's three-month threshold of sick absence on full pay. This was the first I had heard of this reduction in my salary. I had not even been made aware that it was a possibility. She went on to tell me that the school's governors had no discretion in the matter (a statement which I knew at the time to be untrue and which she later retracted) and that I would remain on half pay until such time as I returned to work. After a rather heated exchange, I left the meeting declaring that on that basis, and because I simply could not afford to be on half pay, I would have to return to work immediately after the Christmas break, i.e., the first week in January.

It was just days after the effects of my final chemotherapy session had subsided and I was still awaiting the scan that would tell me if the months of treatment had been a success or not. The prospect of having to have more treatment was still very real, as was the possibility that my match may be over. Yet here I was facing an impossible and unresolvable financial predicament and the prospect of being forced to return to work far earlier than my body and mind were ready for, and against the very clear advice of my consultant. From the moment I left that meeting my anxiety levels increased to new stratospheric heights. The anger I was feeling was almost uncontrollable.

It does not take an economist to work out that a

single parent, caring for three small children, cannot survive on half a teacher's salary. My rent alone took up nearly half of my full earnings. How could I possibly pay my rent, feed my children, pay my bills, and run my car – something I had become increasingly reliant upon as my body had crumbled and become progressively incapable of getting from room to room within my house, never mind getting the children to school or going to the shops to get food – on just half my salary? To add insult to injury, in a wonderfully timed, Patrick-inspired sadistic twist, it was now just one week before Christmas.

Later that day, whilst at home desperately trying to crunch numbers, accurately predict the next set of winning lottery numbers, googling how much a kidney is worth and thinking of ways that I could somehow get myself and my children through this mess, I received a call from the same member of the leadership team. I was still, I think understandably and justifiably, angry about the position she, her manager, the headteacher, and the school had put me in. Despite my resentment, at no point during the conversation did I swear or was I in any way rude or abusive; nevertheless, I was told 'I'd be grateful if you would moderate your tone.' This considerable lack of any kind of understanding, compassion or empathy for my situation was to become the norm over the following months.

The school had created, wholly deliberately, calculatedly and without any compassion, a situation that would ultimately cost me my job, would change my children's education, and therefore their lives, would cause me enormous financial hardship, spiralling debt and court summonses – the consequences of which I am still feeling now, years later – and put me in a position where I was, on more than one occasion, on the very brink of being evicted from my home. This was Patrick at his most vicious.

Over the course of the next few weeks a large number of emails were exchanged between me and school. I tried to seek an explanation, an understanding, of why they had decided not to apply some discretion to my somewhat exceptional circumstances and permit me to remain on full pay for the duration of my absence from school. Their response was that it was a 'business decision' and they wanted to avoid 'creating a precedent' for the future. I still wonder what kind of precedent they were seeking to avoid. A precedent of caring for and supporting a member of staff who has just finished six months of chemotherapy? Even now I struggle to understand how that would be a bad thing. There can be few things an employer can say that are more devastating and demoralising, particularly when faced with a traumatic, physically crushing and debilitating set of circumstances, than that your future welfare and wellbeing was decided on the basis of a 'business decision'.

During this incredibly difficult time, I sent a somewhat misguided email to a very small number of mums at school who I was helping with a netball team they had established. Being involved with this group, although physically difficult, gave me something to do on my 'good' days, made me feel useful and meant that I could maintain some connection with the school. The email was sent a couple of days after I had been informed of the school's decision to cripple me financially, and while the anger, disappointment, frustration and desperation that I was feeling about that decision were still at their zenith. In it I explained the position the school had put me in and said that their behaviour 'certainly isn't very Christian'. The school I worked for claims to have a strong Christian ethos. Clearly in this case a 'Christian ethos' did not extend to not ruining an employee's life and those of his children, and certainly did not involve behaving with any compassion, sympathy or understanding of a fellow human being's distress.

One of the recipients of my email thought it appropriate to copy it to my headteacher. I would have thought that the appropriate action at that point would have been for the Head to simply speak to me about it, say, 'Come on, Ian, I understand your position and how difficult things are for you [which, of course, he wouldn't have done. He would have had absolutely no idea], but sending this kind of message isn't okay', and that be the end of it. That isn't what happened. Instead, the school's senior management were informed, without my knowledge, and a formal disciplinary procedure instigated.

The first I knew of what had happened was upon receipt of a letter from school in the post at home.

The letter began:

'Dear Ian
I am writing to call you to a disciplinary meeting once you are fit to return to work on either a full or part-time basis.'

Details of the allegations were outlined. The letter continued:

'As you are currently on sick leave, I do not consider it appropriate to hold the meeting until you are fit to return to work.'

So, in addition to still facing the very real possibility that my chemotherapy had been unsuccessful and I would either have to embark on another course of treatment or the prognosis was that I would become one of the thirty percent, facing intolerable, inescapable and potentially life-changing financial difficulties, I now also faced the worry and stress of a disciplinary hearing at school, the possible outcome of which, I was told, could be dismissal.

Despite my assertion that I would go back to work far earlier than was advisable, a return at the beginning of January was not possible. The school, having put me in this impossible financial predicament, was now refusing to allow me to return to work, referring to the earlier communication from my consultant advising that I should not return before Easter.

I was wedged between a very big rock, on which Patrick sat, a rather smug spectator, and an extremely hard place. Although he was finding this new situation highly amusing, even Patrick seemed rather bemused by the whole thing. Our adventure had taken an unexpected turn and he looked rather perplexed and more than a little annoyed by this unforeseen development. He sat consulting his map, considering just where we had taken a wrong turn and deviated from his very carefully prepared route.

'Wow, Fry, this is fucked up. This is even more weird than I'd planned. I did not see that coming,' he chuckled, without even a modicum of sympathy.

I now had to turn my attention to the task of somehow getting back to work. I returned to Dr Clark on more than one occasion to request she write to school to enable me to return to work earlier than the date she had initially planned for me.

Dr Clark initially maintained the view that I was not fit enough to return to work, reminding school of the time it takes to recover from intensive chemotherapy, the difficulties my body would have in adjusting to going back to work, and the danger of infection given my immune deficiency. It is difficult to imagine any place, other than a hospital, where germs and viruses are more rife than in a primary school. Being back at school was going to be potentially dangerous for me.

The school maintained their position of keeping me on half pay. I was therefore reduced to having to beg Dr Clark to allow me to return to work. She eventually succumbed to my pleadings and wrote again to school. She was forced into the position of having to explain to my employer that for my overall wellbeing she would endorse a return to work earlier than she had originally recommended, because the alternative, i.e., remaining off work on half pay, would have serious and possibly long-term adverse financial repercussions.

THE CANCER'S ALL GONE

A few days later I sat in front of Dr Clark in her consulting room waiting to hear her verdict. She stared intently at her computer screen at my scan pictures – at least I assumed that was what she was looking at so closely. She didn't strike me as a YouTube cat video watcher. She slowly turned her chair, looked me in the eye and, as a little smile spread across her face, said, 'It worked. The cancer's all gone.'

'Bollocks!' Patrick screamed from his usual position on the bed. 'Bollocks, bollocks, bollocks. I can't believe the treatment worked! After all the time I've invested in this!' He jumped down from his lofty perch and, not for the first time, stormed out of the room.

To say he was unhappy would have been one of the greatest understatements since pilot Eric Moody announced to the passengers on his British Airways flight, his plane having suffered the failure of all four of its engines, 'Ladies and gentlemen, this is your captain speaking. We have a small problem.'

Without the distraction of my stroppy little

companion, I was able to try and digest what Dr Clark had just told me. I sat for a moment in silence. It was the strangest of feelings. The goal I had been working towards for seven months had finally been realised. I had received the news I had been wanting to hear above all else during all the hideousness. The very thing that had enabled me to get through it all. This moment had been the one I had imagined during all the days I spent throwing up, through all the pain and all those sleepless nights. All the times when my body was utterly broken, and the hours attached to a machine in the Sunshine Room. This had been the dream.

I had long imagined being given this news; it was after all the destination I had set for myself when this journey began. I had envisioned the euphoria I would feel at my success. Being told you are in remission is, of course, a cause for great happiness and relief, a positive moment, and I felt that. However, the fire of initial positivity I felt about the fact that the treatment had been completed successfully was quickly doused by an understanding that there remained a significant statistical chance that Patrick would return.

Therefore, far from feeling a sense of relief or celebration, I felt rather numb. Somewhat empty. Which is perhaps rather more literal than figurative in this case, given I no longer had cells I had before the process began. Having had something – cancer, chemotherapy, Patrick – dominate one's life so totally for such a long time, to then have it removed with the utterance of the words 'You're in remission' is extremely odd, almost disconcerting.

It feels, I imagine, having never been kidnapped, a little like Stockholm Syndrome. Patrick had held me hostage for the last seven months and, now that I had been released from his evil clutches and was free, I actually felt rather lost. What was my purpose now? How would I structure my days? What would life be like without Patrick? Who would I turn to for help now that I would no longer be attending the hospital on a bi-weekly basis?

The reality of the situation was, of course, that I was never on my own. Dr Clark, and the other wonderful hospital staff who had always been there for me throughout my journey, made it very clear they would continue to be available to see or chat to if I had any concerns. I would also be having regular check-ups. Nevertheless, I still felt strangely cast adrift from Patrick's island. I was free, but my liberty had come at a price. I was unsure who I was now or what I was now going to do. I had to get my life back on track. I had to try to restore all those things Patrick had taken from me – my health, my identity, my dignity, my relationship with my children.

'How exactly do you plan on doing that?' Patrick shouted angrily from the island as I slowly drifted away.

'I don't know, but I'll be fine,' came my knee-jerk, defiant reaction.

The truth was I had absolutely no idea how I was going to do that. Not even the slightest inkling. Yes, I was free, but everything still seemed very much out of my control.

I was now floating aimlessly away from the Isle of Patrick, destination unknown, in a boat devoid of a rudder or oars and without a map, compass or any other means of navigating this particular course. A boat that before too long would spring a fairly significant leak, and I would find myself bailing out water and paddling frantically back to the only piece of dry land accessible to me – the Isle of Patrick.

Nevertheless, I was in remission. After seven months, four surgical procedures, ten MRI/CT/PET CT scans, twelve chemotherapy sessions, seventy-six and a half hours in the Sunshine Room, fourteen consultations with doctors, twelve visits from district nurses, and having taken 813 pills, I was finally free of Patrick. The double act was over, never to be seen again. No reunion, not even a Christmas Special. Or so I thought.

YOU'RE FIRED

I remained off work for a few more weeks while I travelled to and from the hospital desperately trying to resolve the situation and obtain something that the school would accept to enable me to return. I eventually went back to work at least two months earlier than my consultant had suggested was appropriate for me.

Within forty-eight hours of my return a disciplinary meeting was held. I had always acknowledged that the email I sent was misguided, but I attempted to put that decision in the context of my treatment, my anxieties about the scan results, and the severe financial predicament I faced.

My pleadings fell on deaf ears, and I was given a final written warning.

Patrick was waiting for me in the car. His summation of the situation was brief but to the point: 'WOW!' Even he was incredulous.

This decision had a huge impact on me at a time when I was attempting to restart my life. I found myself working for an employer who clearly had no regard for me or my wellbeing and lacked any appreciation of what I had been through and the situation I was in.

I made a formal appeal against the decision to issue me with a final written warning. During that minuted appeal hearing I was told, 'off the record', that 'my mood was having an adverse effect on my colleagues'! Patrick just sat in the corner of the room shaking his head in disbelief as this almost comical example of how to demonstrate an overwhelming lack of sympathy and understanding to your employee was played out in front of him.

The struggles I faced over the next few months resulted in a drop in the extremely high standards I had always worked to prior to my treatment. I found it incredibly difficult to organise my workload and my memory suffered, resulting in things not getting done on time. These internal struggles were exacerbated by having to work for an employer who had betrayed me in such a spectacular fashion.

This came to a head a couple of months after I had returned to work full time when I was informed I would face another disciplinary. The allegation this time was that there had been a 'lack of marking', 'not setting homework' (on one occasion), and there had been a drop in the 'level of teaching'. I fully accepted that *some* work had gone unmarked. The evidence provided by school consisted of *one* example of not setting homework, an allegation I was never asked about at the time of the said 'offence', and the drop in my levels of teaching was quite clearly a result of everything that had gone before.

During the disciplinary hearing I sought to explain that the chemotherapy had resulted in a condition known as 'chemo brain'. This rather comical label is more formally defined as mild cognitive impairment (MCI), a consequence of intensive chemotherapy. 'Chemo brain' had severely affected my ability to organise my thoughts, my work and my working day effectively. Things got missed because of the chaos and anarchy that ruled my head.

I presented my employer with some of the many published works on post remission issues and the longer-term effects of chemotherapy that explained the consequences of this condition and the effects it would have on my work. I also had letters from my consultant and solicitor confirming MCI. My employers elected to ignore all this irrefutable medical evidence. The result of the disciplinary was that I was dismissed from my position at the school.

A rather burly male member of staff was summoned to escort me to and from my classroom while I collected and packed all my personal belongings and years' worth of accumulated teaching resources into my car until I had left the premises. I was not permitted the opportunity to say goodbye to my colleagues or the children I taught.

I had suffered six months of chemotherapy, had to deal with the tears of my children while they explained they didn't want me to die, confronted head-on the very real prospect I would be dead in a year, experienced pain and discomfort of the kind I had never experienced before and hope never to again. I had spent months coping with an utterly broken body, and numerous nights sleeping downstairs because the physical exertion of getting to my bedroom was too much. I'd thrown up outside the school gates and Asda in the city centre, faced the very real prospect of being evicted, had to wank into a cup to ensure that fathering more children remained an option for me, not to mention the many other associated indignities that Patrick introduced into my life. Despite all this, driving home that day I felt like I had reached a whole new low. There was rock bottom, twenty-five layers of Patrick-induced crap, and then me. I had lost my job because of my inability to cope sufficiently well with my chemotherapy, its aftermath and all the mental turmoil Patrick had created.

'I don't know what to say,' Patrick said almost sympathetically as we drove home. 'This has got way out of hand now.'

I think in his heart of hearts he wanted to apologise for this latest instalment in his chemotherapy box set of shit. He didn't.

THEY THINK IT'S ALL OVER

As well as the immediate emotions surrounding the declaration that I was in remission, there came, even more unexpectedly, a number of post chemotherapy events for which I was not in any way prepared. I had, rather ignorantly as it transpired, entered into this process with the notion that successfully completing the course of chemotherapy would be the end of the matter.

Option one of the three I had considered at the beginning.

During my extensive reading about all matters cancer, I discovered an edited version of a talk given to the annual conference of Cancer Self-Help Groups in 2014 by Dr Peter Harvey, Clinical Psychologist, Leeds Teaching Hospitals Trust.

This article was a real godsend for me, and it was one of those I presented to my employer as part of my disciplinary hearing. It encapsulated perfectly a lot of the feelings, difficulties and issues I was experiencing post chemotherapy.

His talk entitled 'After the Treatment Finishes –

Then What?' begins with Dr Harvey comparing having cancer with a rollercoaster in the following way:

'On a rollercoaster, you will be strapped in and sent off into the terror, knowing there is nothing you can do about it until you emerge, wobbly and battered at the other end. You manage by getting your head down and dealing with it as best you can at the time. It is only afterwards, when you are on solid ground again, that you can look back with amazement and view what you have experienced and marvel at your courage.'

Dr Harvey's analogy describes what happens after diagnosis and treatment. The end of the rollercoaster ride is equivalent to the end of the treatment. He then goes on to explain that this is likely to be far from being the end.

'After the treatment has finished and at the point where you can begin, bit-by-bit, to deal with all that you have been through and all that is to come. You may have had to endure months of treatment by knife, chemicals or radiation until you are probably sick of the whole business, both literally and metaphorically. Now is the time to heal, both body and mind.'

Very little of what I had read prior to this article dealt with the post-treatment stage. Everyone involved – medical staff, friends, family, and even me – in some ways understandably, had been utterly transfixed on reaching November 20th and (hopefully) going into remission. No one had prepared me for what was to follow. I walked blindly ignorant into the promised land of remission, without any real understanding of what awaited me there.

Dr Harvey talks about the importance of establishing a 'framework' to develop the understanding of what is happening and what is going to happen. The first part of the framework is the recovery process, which he subdivides into three stages: recuperation, convalescence and rehabilitation.

As Mollie very quickly and very astutely, and in an incredibly dismissive 'don't be so silly, Daddy' kind of way that all parents will be familiar with, pointed out, it made absolutely no sense for the doctors to give me medicine that would actually make me feel worse. Doctors are, after all, supposed to make you feel better, not worse, she argued. It was a contention I found impossible to argue with. I could of course have ventured into a quasi-medical discussion with her about how cancerous cells are dealt with, but I was content to let my seven-year-old win the argument, primarily, of course, because she was right – something which I am learning very quickly will evidently happen more and more as my girls grow up.

The fact that it is the treatment rather than the cancer itself that makes you poorly, certainly initially at least and most definitely in the way portrayed in all the cancer-related advertising, is 'one of the many paradoxes of cancer'. This is because, as Dr Clark pointed out to me during our first meeting, the aggressiveness of the treatment is a necessary response to the power of the disease, but it is the power of the treatments that cause such huge physical strains on the body. Combine this power, aggression and the poisons being used to treat cancer patients and you very quickly end up with a repugnant cocktail of factors that combine to create the hideousness that is cancer treatment. The situation is exacerbated by the fact that there is often little time to recover from one treatment before the next one starts. I remember all too well how the joy and relief I felt during those few days in each two week-cycle were tempered with the realisation that within a matter of days I would be riding the chemotherapy rollercoaster once more.

In addition to the fact that your body is being pumped full of toxins, Dr Harvey explains the other reasons why chemotherapy has the effect it does:

'The treatments themselves may make it difficult to sleep and eat properly – two important parts of the body's defence and recovery system. Some of the treatments drain your energy and resources to such an extent that it's as much as you can do to put on the kettle. Add to this the emotional turmoil – the dealing with the impact and implications of the diagnosis, the uncertainty, the upheaval, the additional burden that you feel that you are imposing on family and friends, the loss of so many aspects of your routine. Emotional stress can be as energy consuming as any physical activity. After all. Is it any wonder that you feel wrung out and exhausted, without resources or reserves?'

The next stage of Dr Harvey's framework is convalescence. This is simply the process of growing strong again, and getting back to the physical levels you were at prior to your diagnosis and treatment. For me this involved a desire just to rest. Although I had spent the previous seven months pretty much just sitting on my arse doing bugger all, that was an imposed state of inertia, something forced upon me by Patrick. It was also time I spent a majority of in pain. What I wanted was to be able to relax without the pain and the anxiety. I wanted to be able to relax properly. To read again for pleasure rather than simply as a mechanism intended to try and take my mind off the pain, although as a painkiller it was never the best. I wanted to be able to get to a point in the day when I was tired and looked forward to sleeping, not going to sleep afraid that I might be awoken in the night by pain in my legs, my arms, my mouth or because I had wet the bed. I wanted to sleep a restful sleep, not one constantly interrupted by the thoughts and emotions swirling around my head. I wanted to sleep without feeling guilty about the fact that by not staying awake I was potentially wasting what might only be a few more months before I was finally overcome by Patrick's tyranny, and the sense I should be doing something more useful. Given that it took every modicum of energy I had to put my socks on every day, I am not sure exactly what it is I thought I would do instead of sleeping, but I'm fairly certain that whatever it was wasn't going to happen.

I CAN'T AFFORD TO FEED MY CHILDREN

There were many consequences to my relationship with Patrick. Some of which I foresaw, some of which I most certainly did not.

Losing my job as a direct result of my chemotherapy and its aftereffects was the most unexpected of all the things that happened to me during that time. The treatment I experienced at the hands of my employer unnecessarily and significantly hindered my efforts at recuperation following the completion of my treatment. I was put in a position where I was having to deal with legal issues, on an almost daily basis, instead of focussing on getting my mind and body back into something like the condition they were in prior to Patrick's arrival.

Although his primary objective to kill me had failed, his lack of success had come with a surprise bonus. A consolation prize. A prize he accepted with much glee, despite his initial incredulity.

No information was ever provided to my colleagues, parents or the wider school community explaining the reason for my sudden departure. Such an information void is the perfect breeding ground for gossip, rumours and lies. These rumours, often salacious, all inaccurate, were impossible for me to refute and have resulted in unresolved and ongoing damage to both my personal and professional reputation that continues to adversely affect my everyday life, even years later.

Of even more immediate significance was the financial predicament in which I found myself. It was impossible for me to live in anything like a manageable way. Overnight my income had been halved, yet I still had all the same bills and outgoings. I think even Patrick was embarrassed by my situation, which he had indirectly caused, although he was now as powerless as me to influence matters.

On more than one occasion I got to the till at Tesco having managed to get around the shop without succumbing to the need to stop and rest – progress indeed – only to be told that my card had been declined because of insufficient funds. I can think of very few occasions in my life when I have been more embarrassed than when having to explain to one of the checkout staff at my local supermarket that I didn't have enough money to pay for the basket of food I had presented her with, and then having to walk out empty handed leaving my shopping – food for my children's school lunches – and my dignity behind. The shame of not being able to afford groceries for my family was crushingly embarrassing.

What kind of father can't even provide for his children?

'They're your children, Fry. You're supposed to provide for them,' was Patrick's very unsympathetic but nevertheless accurate take on matters as I walked, utterly ashamed, back to my car.

'I'm very aware of that,' I snapped, 'but whose fault is it that I can't provide for them?'

'Actually, this time, it isn't mine,' Patrick replied somewhat defensively.

He wasn't wrong.

This spectacular failure represented yet another massive undermining of the foundations upon which my role as Daddy was built, to add to all the other failures my children had already endured during the previous months. As a father, not being able to provide for my children was devastating and humiliating in the extreme.

As my debts spiralled out of control I considered robbing a bank, but was concerned about my ability to stand for long enough to convince a cashier in my local TSB to hand over the cash. No one is going to feel too threatened by a bloke having to pause halfway through his demands to sit down to take a breather. I was also unconvinced about how useful Patrick would be in this situation. A teddy bear in school uniform doesn't exactly scream gangster.

Having dismissed the prospect of a lucrative life of crime as a realistic possibility for me and Patrick, I was forced to take just about the only course available to me. I resorted to taking out payday loans so I could buy food and pay my rent. This is, of course, a very short fix which actually causes far greater long-term problems. I knew that before I took that decision, but I had no choice.

Twice during this period I was served with an eviction notice from my landlord because I had been unable to make the monthly rental payments. It was either payday loans or we didn't eat and got evicted.

I did receive a little relief from MacMillan and a local cancer charity, who both gave me financial gifts. I cannot even begin to put into words how much those gestures of support meant to me at the time and still do now. Without their support I would certainly have been evicted. Financially, of course, their kindness and generosity helped, if only for a short time, but it was the gesture behind the gifts that I found most heart-warming. Just knowing there was someone out there who was willing to help me meant so much at a time when I was floundering uncontrollably, alone. I was, once again, buried deep in the snow, desperately in need of a shovel.

I spent months, both before and after my dismissal, consulting with solicitors, lodging an ultimately unsuccessful appeal against my dismissal with school, attempting to resolve the situation as satisfactorily for me as I could. The uncertainty, pressure and anxiety caused by such legal wranglings took a significant toll on me both mentally and physically. It prevented me from recuperating in the way I should have done after my treatment and just prolonged the anguish far further than it needed to or should have been.

THE BEST THING THAT EVER HAPPENED TO ME

Being told I had a thirty percent chance that I'd be dead in a year had a profound emotional and psychological impact on me, although most of that reaction came very late in the process. The very stark reality that all the assumptions I had made about my life – being able to watch my children grow up; the people I'd be close to; all the places and things I was yet to experience – could become a mere fantasy was a very difficult thing to get my head around. It resonated in a unique way, becoming, for a while at least, a tumultuous hurricane of thoughts and emotions, before finding its way into all the nooks and crannies of my being and becoming all consuming.

Very early on in my journey with Patrick I read a quote from a woman who insisted, without any sense of irony or sarcasm, that 'having cancer might be the best thing that ever happened to me'. She acknowledged that this statement was made with the obvious caveat that if her cancer was to kill her then that statement would prove not to be true. She explained: 'With the cancer diagnosis, my priorities changed in an instant. The list of what was truly important got real short, real quick.'

I read other very similar declarations from a significant number of other cancer sufferers. These people differed in age, gender, ethnicity, faith and even life expectancy, but had one thing in common: a declared belief that being told 'You have cancer' was, or had become, in some bizarre way, a positive.

One commentator explained that 'cancer improved my life and made me a better man', while another declared that 'cancer changed my attitude to everything'. Others opined how having cancer and going through treatment had made them reflect on their lives and encouraged them to make things better for themselves. One woman proclaimed that, once her treatment was complete, she was going to move house, quit her job and divorce her husband. (I can only assume she had not discussed any of this with him.)

Whilst I understood the thinking behind these seemingly drastic life-changing decisions, such radical action was not for me, primarily because Patrick had seen to it that I certainly couldn't afford to move home, I loved my job, and I didn't have a partner to get rid of.

I read many of these quotes at an early stage in my treatment while I was still coming to terms with all the sickness, fatigue and truck hitting. At that time the suggestion that having cancer was in any way a positive thing seemed utterly preposterous. Off-the-scale ridiculous. How can having a condition that might kill you and the treatment for which induces months of misery be a positive? These people were all clearly certifiable. However, as time has gone on, and particularly now that my journey with Patrick is over, I have come to a very similar conclusion, although I suspect for rather different reasons.

Having cancer and going through chemotherapy, with all its delightful medical, physiological and psychological consequences, is unquestionably a life-defining experience. Cancer and all its associated repugnance changes people. They are never the same as they were prior to their diagnosis.

I am no exception. Sharing my life with Patrick for seven months certainly changed me. Whilst I cannot, unfortunately, honestly profess that my relationship with Patrick made me a better man, I am most definitely a different man. Patrick has altered my attitude to everything, and my priorities have changed significantly.

Patrick has transformed my outlook on life, my habits, my attitude towards others, my awareness of my own mortality. I appreciate things, almost everything, in a way I never did before. I am even more opinionated and less tolerant than I was BP (Before Patrick), which those who knew me BP will confirm is quite an achievement. The wonder of nature inspires me even more than it did before my treatment, and I want to travel and see new places in a way I never did before. Whilst acknowledging that my work as a teacher remains as important as it was BP, I have realised that it does not define me. Patrick made me realise that as much as I love teaching and am passionate about the small role I can play in nurturing, developing and hopefully making a positive difference to the children in my care, not even this role can compete, nor would it again ever be allowed to compete with the needs of my children. Never again would I work such long hours, both at school and at home, and compromise my quality time with the Small Frys. I now know that the only thing in my life that really matters is my children. Everything else pales into insignificance against the needs of those three precious people.

So considerable was the affect Patrick had on my life I even joined a gym! But that particular consequence was one that most definitely didn't last very long.

Living with Patrick was not the end of my life, nor was it the beginning of a new life, it was simply my life, interrupted.

More than anything Patrick made me realise that I don't want to die. A fairly obvious and pre-conditioned desire for most; a rather radical change of perspective for me.

THANKS, PATRICK

I have suffered from and lived with severe clinical depression for forty-plus years. In the years prior to meeting Patrick, I had three serious nervous breakdowns and received years of psychiatric and psychological help, support and intervention from an army of mental health experts.

I have consumed a ridiculous number of anti-depressants, some of which worked, some didn't. Some made me hallucinate. Others gave me an appetite so voracious I ate almost constantly. Others made me sick, while some made me so tired I found it literally impossible to stay awake regardless of where I was. I stopped driving for fear of falling asleep at the wheel, and I had to refrain from sitting down at any point during my working day in order to stay awake, although I am sure, given time, I could have perfected the art of sleeping standing up.

Many times, the oppressive, enveloping, suffocating darkness that has consumed me and my life has made the prospect of continuing to live as me completely intolerable. The overriding sensation was one of simply needing it to stop and being prepared to do whatever it took to make that happen. During those four decades I had more serious thoughts of suicide than I can possibly count. On several occasions I had stockpiled the pills I intended to take and written goodbye letters.

My last massive breakdown prompted my wife to ring our insurance company to find out if my life insurance would still be paid if I killed myself, so convinced was she that everything had become too much for me and I would end it all.

I was, and in many ways remain, utterly and irreparably mentally broken. I have always described my depression as like living life standing on a trap door. On a good day the trap door remains firmly closed, ably supporting my weight enabling me to get on with my life. On a bad day the door collapses beneath me without warning and I plummet into the void below. If I'm lucky I land on a ledge where I remain until I find the strength to extricate myself. If the ledge is missed, I plunge deeper and deeper into the darkness below. With no obvious way out or means of escape I remain enveloped in the increasingly grim terrifyingly oppressive nothingness.

Living in a constant state of apprehension and ignorance of the trap door's ability to remain closed on any given day is hard work. The daily façade I have developed over many, many years has been perfected to the extent I am fairly confident that almost everyone who has ever met me would have little idea of the turmoil going on in my head. However, this pretence comes at a price. It is utterly exhausting.

Prior to the arrival of Patrick, my depression

affected every aspect of my life. My breakdowns caused my body, both physically and mentally, to shut down. I would spend days not getting dressed, not eating, barely functioning at all, sitting in the corner of a room with my knees clutched to my chest in the desperate hope that something or someone would make it stop, take the pain away and release the vice-like grip crushing my head and disperse the torment that paralysed me physically and mentally. I would have done anything to make it stop.

If Lucifer himself had appeared before me offering to bring it all to an end in exchange for my soul and an eternity of damnation, I would have bitten his hand off. Time without end in perdition with Beelzebub, the evil dead and all the punitive suffering and torture, was most certainly a favourable alternative to the life I was living. Given that Satan is no more real that Patrick, and the selling of my soul was not an option, I was left with only one escape route. One means of ending the torment – suicide.

In my earlier years something within me prohibited the taking of that most final of courses. It may have been cowardice (suicide is after all an incredibly brave thing to do). Perhaps I regarded it as fundamentally objectionable given that many people live lives far harder than mine was or ever has been. I can't honestly say what it was that prevented me from seeking that most permanent of escape routes from the pain, but I didn't.

More recently the option of permanent release from the torment has been taken away by my sense of loyalty and the consuming love I have for my children. I could not and would not swap my pain for theirs. No matter how impossible things seem for me, doing anything that would intentionally take their dad away from them was simply not an option. I could not deliberately cause them that anguish. Nevertheless, the desire to make things stop remained all too real. The overriding feeling I had was one of hopelessness. I just could not do it anymore. Being me was too hard, but the Small Frys meant that ending it all was no longer an option. In many ways I resented the change in my available choices.

Patrick changed that. The prospect of becoming one of the thirty percent convinced me that although things were difficult, in many ways indescribably difficult, Patrick made me realise I did not want it to end. He gave me a determination to go on regardless of how shit things were. The realisation that Patrick could kill me simply made me determined to stick around.

The decision as to whether or not I continued my presence at the party of life was now no longer a matter of consideration for me alone. The choice had, again, been taken away from me, but this time under duress. Patrick had snatched it out of my grasp and claimed it as his own. He was my chief tormentor elect, desperate to usurp depression as the undisputed champion. He and only he could now decide for how much longer I lived. This time, however, the removal of choice changed my perspective in a positive way. Patrick was now in control. I wasn't having that. If I was going to die it would be when I say, on my terms, not Patrick's, and at forty-three I certainly wasn't ready to check out yet.

My depression continues at the same levels it always has. The daily grind persists. Every day is a struggle of differing degrees, some far more difficult than others, and I continue to live each day encased behind a mask of pretence and supported by a huge amount of daily medication, without which everything would be impossible. Although there are many days when I just want the crushing lows to stop and to find some light and escape the darkness, one thing has changed: I know now that no matter how bad it gets, and how much I want the world to stop so I can get off, I no longer want to die.

I still spend my days standing somewhat precariously atop my rather rickety and particularly unreliable trap door. However, the work Patrick did on repairing the dilapidated lock mechanism means that my position is rather more secure than it ever has been. That does not mean I don't have days when I once again, without notice, find myself falling into the darkness. Now though the ledge is wider than it ever was and, if I look up towards the light, I see Patrick's little face peering down at me and a paw reaching out ready to haul me back to the real world – a world I continue to find all too frequently unbearable, but one Patrick has made me realise I would rather live in, with the pain in my head and the unrelenting torment, than not be here at all.

The Patrick-facilitated recalibration of my mind has fixed me, albeit in a rather unconventional, very precarious, held-together-by-Sellotape kind of way. Patrick has given me a newfound desire to stick around, and for that I will always be grateful.

QED: Patrick = The best thing that ever happened to me (apart from the Small Frys).

UNDATABLE

The time Patrick and I spent together changed my attitude to a huge number of things. Some of them extremely profound, others far less important.

One of the first things I did once my chemo had finished was to enrol with an online dating agency. I'd never previously had any desire to join those who were already part of the huge online dating revolution. Now, having spent the last seven months exclusively with Patrick, I felt the need to find someone else to spend my time with, preferably someone who didn't try to destroy my life. I no longer came as part of a rather unsavoury, dysfunctional pair. It was just me.

Meeting people on these websites was becoming the new norm. Prior to Patrick's arrival it was not a method I had ever subscribed to, but times were changing, as was I.

However, enrolling on the online site was less of a declaration of my entrance to the new technological age and more a recognition that, thanks to Patrick, I felt significantly less datable than I had ever done before. I still had my 'magic tubes' sticking out of my chest, a drooping eye, several chemo/biopsy scars, significant mental hangover, not to mention the very attractive bald patches on the back of my legs. These charming features combined to make me feel like something out of *The Undatables*.

Good luck, match.com.

Unperturbed by such obvious handicaps, and determined to take back control of my life in a more significant and substantive way than simply being stroppy with nursing staff or ignoring medical advice, I completed a dating profile and paid the subscription fee.

The next few months were, on reflection, some of the strangest of my life, which is quite a claim given the adventures Patrick and I had been through. Online dating was, even by the standards of my last seven months, the most surreal experience.

It was often incredibly frustrating. Rejections are, of course, a fundamental part of the online dating process, I knew that, but nevertheless the rejections I experienced, from women I had never even met and who did not know me, fuelled the more negative feelings about myself that were one of Patrick's less noticeable legacies.

The process was not without its positives. It was frequently a cause for some much-needed laughter. But some of the people I encountered were beyond weird!

Each of the individual profiles includes a section that asks the subject to outline their 'Dislikes', things they would not accept in a potential partner. These are a genuine selection of the responses to this question in the profiles I saw:

- Would rather not date anyone addicted to crystal meth or a Muslim extremist
- Violence
- Drug addiction
- Bad manners
- Lack of personal hygiene
- Bad breath
- People who abuse and neglect animals
- Hatred
- Racism
- Corruption, liars and thieves
- Alcoholism, violence, ignorance, rudeness
- Psychopaths

We all make strange decisions when relationships end, and occasionally do things that we wouldn't otherwise do and later regret, but I have to admit to floundering in the nutter-infested waters of online dating where this kind of madness seemed entirely normal. What on earth was I doing?

Knowing that such people existed did at least make me feel a lot more normal than I had for an awfully long time and, despite all the insanity, I did meet some very nice women. I only had four dates, but three of them progressed beyond that first date phase.

The exception was a beautiful woman to whom I was very attracted, but who, towards the end of our dinner date, received what I can only assume was a 'rescue call' giving her the option to get the hell out of there. She took it.

This was the world that Patrick had forced me into. A world of frustration, disappointment and complete madness. He and his occupying army had been driven out, but not before booby trapping the land he had dominated, making it as difficult as possible for me to return to a normal life, leaving me in a state of paranoia long after he had gone.

As I drove home from the restaurant that night, alone, I had some very stern words for Patrick. It was the first time I had spoken to him for a while, and given that I was now in remission, I couldn't be sure he was still with me. I had assumed not, but on that night, and on other occasions when I was reminded of our time together and the issues he continued to cause me, I felt the need to communicate my frustrations and anger to him.

'See what you've made me do? The situation you've put me in! You're not even here anymore but I still have to live with all your crap. You did this, you little shit!'

Although I was sure Patrick was not there with me, I'm convinced I heard a little, almost indiscernible voice in the distance, 'I'll always be with you, Fry, don't you worry about that.'

The other women I met were all utterly delightful. They each helped me enormously to get my life back on track. They made me feel like the old Fry again. They gave me a sense of worth. They enabled me to feel like Ian Fry the man, the person again, rather than Ian Fry, the cancer sufferer. They helped me restore my identity. An identity that Patrick had stripped me of. I was now able to see myself as an individual again and not as one half of the Patrick and Ian double act of which I had been a part for so long.

BYE, PATRICK

As with any break-up at the end of a relationship of significant length, my split from Patrick was not without its difficulties. My little furry friend and I had spent the best part of a year together. It had, like most relationships, had its intense moments. We'd been through some of the most bizarre things together, and we'd cried (at least I had).

The time and adventures we shared had been one of the most important, significant and influential periods of my life. We had some interesting times, and saw and did some things I had never experienced in any other relationship I'd been in. We'd even had a few laughs as we shared some genuinely ludicrous moments.

Nevertheless, our relationship had run its course and it was time to say goodbye. Like most relationships it came to an end for a number of different reasons. I could have had the stereotypical 'it's not you, it's me' conversation with him, but like most people who attribute that reasoning to their break-up, I would have been lying. It most definitely wasn't me. It was him. He was spiteful, sadistic, selfish, irritating, impossible to live with, a pain in the arse and I couldn't wait to get shot of him.

Primarily, though, our departure came about due to one fundamental difference of opinion: Patrick wanted to kill me, and I didn't want him to.

I had always hoped, and indeed expected, that the success of the treatment I had received would signal an end to my relationship with Patrick. I would be able to vacate the island and get on with my life back on the mainland. However, the legal and financial ramifications of my treatment at the hands of my employers meant that Patrick had stuck around, desperate, I'm sure, to be told that the additional stresses and anxieties would enable him to once again take over my life. For a while we continued to live together on the island as part of some carcinogenic trial separation.

After months of this sleeping-in-separate-rooms kind of cohabiting, the conclusion of matters relating to my employment meant that we finally reached the point where Patrick and I had to make the separation permanent and go our different ways.

The time had come to say goodbye. Moving out day had finally arrived. I could make my way from the Isle of Patrick, which had been my home for the last ten months, back to the mainland. Back to the normality I had yearned to be part of again for so long.

There was no welcoming party, no shouts and cheers from well-wishers greeting my return from my travels, no fireworks or flares. Instead, I was met by a sea of apathy. Just people going about their everyday lives still utterly oblivious to me, who I was and why I was there.

As I finally stepped out of my boat and set foot once again on the banks of the river I had gazed at with such envy whilst imprisoned on Patrick's island, I turned and glanced back at my former home. Everything about it looked so different from this vantage point. From my new far less stressful perspective, the Isle of Patrick had a completely different look and feel. It was remarkable just how pleasant and tranquil it looked from this viewpoint.

I could see Patrick standing on the shore near the point from which I had boarded my boat, at the end of the little beach he had taken me to on my first day on the island. He looked sad. In all our time together I had never seen him look like that. He had always been the strength in our relationship. He was the dominant, controlling force. The instigator, the organiser. He was the energy and he always seemed very content in his role. Now he seemed lost.

I stood there for a few moments not knowing what to do. I had become accustomed to not doing anything without Patrick's permission. I felt like a well-trained dog waiting for his master's instructions, refusing to budge until the order came.

For ten long months I had yearned for this day. The day when I could leave the Isle of Patrick and resume my own life on the mainland. Now the time had arrived, and I was being left to my own devices, it was far more difficult than I had ever imagined it would be. I had become so adjusted to living on Patrick's whim, that I now felt rather cast adrift and alone. I had been a pawn in Patrick's game, a game I never understood the rules for, and I wasn't sure I knew how to make my own decisions about my life anymore and control the destiny of the game myself.

I stood, unable to move, staring across the water to my former companion. The distance that now separated us made him appear so very tiny. He was standing next to the 'Isle of Patrick' population sign. The '2' he had added to reflect my move to the island all those months ago had been crossed through and a '1' written next to it.

Alone, against the backdrop of his island, he now had an air of vulnerability. It was hard to imagine how something so small could have been the cause of so much misery. We stood mirroring each other in our immobility. There was an apparent shared reluctance for either of us to make the final move that would bring the curtain down on our union.

Patrick was first to accept the inevitable. With a wave of his little paw, and what I am sure was the glimmer of a smile, he turned and slowly walked away from the shore. He was quickly out of sight, consumed by the trees and shrubbery of his island. He was gone.

THE NEVER-ENDING JOURNEY

It has been many months since Patrick turned and disappeared into the darkness of his island. Nevertheless, the consequences of our relationship are still apparent in almost every facet of my life and evident in almost everything I do, try as I might not to think about him. There is a Patrick-shaped hole in the garden fence of my life.

As the months since his departure have passed the hole has gradually been filled with the new growth of the surrounding plant life, but the outline of his shape can still be made out, a permanent memorial to our time together.

In addition to the metaphorical hole in my fence, Patrick left other, very real, physical reminders of our relationship. My right arm is still very sensitive to touch because of the damage done to the veins during the intravenous chemo sessions, and my body bears the marks from the operations and other medical procedures Patrick made me have. These scars from my scraps with him are worn with no little amount of pride, like badges of honour representing my time with him.

Intensive chemo can cause long-term immune deficiency. Whilst my levels remain lower than they would otherwise have been, it is not something that causes me any practical difficulties. It is recommended that I have an annual flu jab, which I do, but otherwise it has no tangible effect on my life.

Regaining any sort of fitness has been incredibly difficult after spending seven months sitting on my arse hanging out with Patrick. Although I have tried, if I'm honest, my attempts at regaining my BP fitness levels have not been consistent. I just like doing bugger all too much.

I am no longer permitted to give blood, something I had done since I was eighteen. Although a relatively minor thing in the great scheme of things, it is something I miss doing. Just another item permanently scratched from my list of permissible activities as a result of my adventures with Patrick.

Although more visually obvious, Patrick's physical legacy is much less damaging than the emotional one.

Even after such a long time since we went our separate ways, I experience a number of ongoing psychological effects from my time with Patrick and the treatment I was given, not all of which are bad. Psychologically, many of the consequences of my adventures with Patrick are positive ones.

My children were always the most important thing to me, but Patrick's attempts to cut short our time together reaffirmed their place at the pinnacle of my life and my desire to do everything I can, every day, to ensure they know how much they are loved and cherished, that they are and will always be the most important thing in my life, and to help them along their individual life paths. They continue to grow and develop into wonderful young people, and it is only a matter of sheer good fortune that I am still around to observe and guide them on their journey. I intend to maximise that luck and enjoy them as much as possible.

That said, they still have the capacity to drive me absolutely nuts, irritate me to the point of distraction, and make me consider how much easier my life would be if my swimmers had stopped working many years ago rather than only developing a state of inertia as a result of my chemo. I have been banned from eBay because of my regular attempts to auction the three of them off to the highest bidder. It turns out, I can't even give them away.

My attitude to my work has changed radically. My job has taken a new, far more realistic place in my priorities. I still love my role as a primary school teacher in a different school, as I was determined to stick to the job I love so much, but I now approach it very differently to the way I did before Patrick turned up.

Despite all this significant positivity there are, perhaps not unsurprisingly, elements of my psyche and mental wellbeing that have been affected in a rather more negative way.

Although no one knows for certain how long the effects of 'chemo brain' last, and like all things cancer related, it varies from person to person, I am sure I still suffer from a mild cognitive impairment. Many aspects of my thought processes and cognitive dexterity are nowhere near back to the levels they were prior to my treatment. My ability to maintain sustained levels of concentration is relatively low, my processing skills are not what they were, and my memory sucks – although that isn't such a new thing. A friend and former teaching colleague always referred to me as 'goldfish brain' long before Patrick turned up. I believe that the intensity of the chemotherapy I received is the cause of these issues, but I remain open to the idea that my advancing years may also be a contributory factor.

Since Patrick left, I have become increasingly paranoid about any health issues that arise. I am still as resolute as I always was in the face of physical illness, and I have not become a full-blown hypochondriac, but I am most certainly more conscious of any aches, pains or unusual feelings in my body. The pragmatic part of me, which is the bit that used to exclusively control my decision-making and attitude towards such matters BP, remains audible, telling me consistently it is nothing to worry about and I shouldn't even give it a second thought. However, this message now conflicts with that of 'Paranoid Fry', whose primary view is always that any ailment is irrefutable evidence of Patrick's reappearance, like some terrible sequel, 'The Return of Patrick' or 'Patrick 2 – This Time It's Personal', coming SOON to my own personal cinema.

I have, to date, rebuffed the obsessive urgings of 'Paranoid Fry' to seek medical advice on all bar two occasions. When I did eventually, but rather apologetically, inform my new consultant (Dr Clark had moved on from her role at the Worcester Royal shortly after I completed my treatment), during one of my routine post-chemo check-ups, about an apparent lump that had manifested itself under the skin at the base of my sternum, he was very understanding and agreed that it was absolutely the right thing to do to have reported it to him. He was confident it was nothing to concern us unduly (that was a phrase I'd heard before), but sent me off for a PET CT scan just to make sure.

Attending the same private clinic I had for all my earlier PET CT scans was rather unnerving. Memories of my previous visits with Patrick, and the association with my feelings at the time, came flooding back. Even on the drive to the clinic I began to feel the crushing, oppressive presence of Patrick in the car with me. He never spoke, but it felt very much as if he was there again, almost staking out his ground in preparation for his re-emergence at the vanguard of his occupying army, readying themselves to once again seize control of my life.

His reconnaissance and preparatory manoeuvres were premature. The scan results were clear, and although my consultant was unable to tell me what the lump was, he was able to confirm categorically 'it's not cancer'. I would be lying if I tried to claim that the time between scan and results was anything less than terrifying. The thought of hearing those three little words again and embarking on another adventure with Patrick was impossible to comprehend.

The other review came as a result of the recurrence of the feeling of pressure on my windpipe, the same sensation that had prompted my very first visit to my GP and which had been the catalyst for all the Patrick-filled merriment. I was sent for another scan, this time a CT scan. As part of the scan process I was given a 'contrast' (dye). I'd had such contrasts before without any reaction. This time, however, it made me vomit within minutes of entering my system. The nurse's surprise at my physical reaction – 'It's unusual for patients to actually be sick' – was easily explained. Patrick. This was how pathetic my body had become.

The cloud of Patrick still floats over me, albeit a somewhat smaller, paler, rather less menacing cloud. But as my separation date from Patrick slips ever further into my past, it becomes less and less obvious as it rises higher into the sky and affords more light to shine on my life, but it is always there.

When the protestations of 'Paranoid Fry' are at their loudest, 'Pragmatic Fry' consoles me with the knowledge that statistically I am now no more likely to get cancer than any other non-smoking, occasional drinking, relatively fit man of my age. That understanding is obviously encouraging and to be welcomed, but it does not stop 'Paranoid Fry' occasionally looking up to see Patrick's cloud there, hovering precariously, rather less threateningly than before, but still above my head.

I have always worried that Patrick may find his way directly into the life of the Small Frys. My research into the question of whether or not Hodgkin's lymphoma is hereditary is less than conclusive. The NHS's website states 'Hodgkin's lymphoma isn't thought to run in families. Although your risk is increased if a first degree relative (parent, sibling, child) has had lymphoma. It's not clear if this is because of an inherited genetic fault or lifestyle factors.' So, the answer to my query about the possibility of my children being targeted by Patrick at some point because of a 'genetic fault' inherited from me is 'maybe, maybe not'. Not exactly reassuring.

My 'can he, can't he?' infertility conundrum remains unanswered, because the question has not yet been asked in anything other than a theoretical sense. My sperm remain frozen and stored in the hospital, standing by and fully equipped to answer a call to arms: 'Fry's swimmers are incapable of getting off their arses, we need your help, come (no pun intended) quick!'

I think the chances of me ever needing to call for reinforcements is unlikely, not because I am convinced of the stamina and abilities of the swimmers that remain inside me to perform their one and only function, but because I am rather put off the prospect of fathering another child by the knowledge of just how hard raising children is, and the understanding there is every chance that having Small Fry #4 in my middle age would almost certainly kill me. I had always wanted more children, but I think that particular ship may have sailed. Nevertheless, it is comforting to know that the option is there should I feel the need to put myself through that again.

The profile of the 'Big C' in our society means that we are regularly bombarded with information about cancer. How likely we are to get it and what we can do to help prevent it. I fully support the raising of awareness about the preventative measures we can all take to thwart cancer and the efforts we can make to raise money for those trying to acquire a greater understanding of Patrick and all his little mates. However, I find it incredibly hard to watch or listen to anything that reports the suffering of others. I can't do it. I have no idea how to process and deal with these constant reminders of those whose journey with their own Patrick did not end as well as mine.

Many who have had cancer treatment, and survived

to fight another day, talk of their desire to embrace life post-remission. Although I have not become a 'live each day to the full, make every day count' kind of person, I am certainly more conscious and appreciative of time and life generally than I was before I met Patrick. This epiphany was less profound in me than it is in some. I am still very happy to sit on my arse and do nothing when I feel like it.

After Patrick's departure from my life I met Melissa – 'Liss'. She came along to train with Droitwich Spa Ladies FC. I was instantly attracted to her. She joined the team and not long after we began dating. We have since married. Liss has brought a meaning and an energy to my life. I love the life we have together, and she has certainly made the process of moving on from my last big relationship – with Patrick – so much easier. We do almost everything together. With Liss I have rediscovered a love of travel and have journeyed extensively around Europe and beyond. I am rarely happier than when exploring a foreign city and culture with Liss. She is undoubtedly a far better travel companion than Patrick.

Living with Patrick was a learning curve of the most profound kind. I learnt so much about myself, my children and life in general, and endured, shared and enjoyed a litany of new and hopefully never to be repeated experiences. It was in some ways good practice for what was to follow.

The coronavirus pandemic, the numerous lockdowns to which we were subjected, the suspension of life as we know it and the huge number of deaths, in some ways meant us all having to deal with a Patrick-like phenomenon. For me it was certainly a stark reminder of my adventures with Patrick. My own positive test was for a time very scary. Patrick's demolition of my immune system meant that although I was no more likely to catch the virus than anyone else, the chances of it killing me, given I now have a defence mechanism as effective as a chocolate fireguard, were significantly higher. I was buggered if, having seen off Patrick, I was now going to succumb to Covid-19, although again I had to accept that there was, in reality, as with Patrick, very little I could do about it. I just had to hope it didn't kill me. It didn't, and my period of illness, during which I was fairly poorly, lasted no more than a couple of weeks. In comparison to living with Patrick the Covid-19 lark was a walk in the park.

THE POST-PATRICK ME

Just as Covid-19 has created a worldwide 'new normal', so Patrick did the same for me and the Small Frys. Our new normal consisted of a daddy still ravaged and tormented by the effects of severe depression, but who accepted this was how life was going to be and that my children could be assured I would be around for a long, long time to come, whether their teenage selves liked it or not, until nature decided otherwise. Personal responsibility for my escape from the daily torment was no longer something I would be instigating.

Our new normal consisted of a daddy who had the realisation that nothing was more important than his children rammed home in the most brutal, yet welcoming way. Patrick taught me, unwittingly, that henceforth every decision I made would be based on their best interests. My Post-Patrick (PP) dates were always made aware they would come fourth in my list of priorities after my precious children, and Liss took all four of us on with that strength and energy that continues to be a wonderful part of my life.

Single-minded, determined, principled and resilient are all characteristics that have always applied to me, but since my relationship with Patrick I am all those things in an even more obvious and transparent way. My intolerance of injustice and abuses of power are now even more evident than they were BP.

Whilst there remains part of me that does not give a shit what people think of me, I will not allow lies to be peddled to meet the pre-determined goals of those in positions of authority whose only objective is to undermine and persecute me. I will not allow lies to become the accepted truth simply because it fits in with someone's misguided and completely inaccurate perception of me.

I am now even more vociferous in my questioning of ideas and decisions that I believe to be wrong or disadvantageous for either me, my children, Liss, or those for whom I am responsible in any capacity. I have never been a 'yes man', but my relationship with Patrick has increased my determination to defend my principles. Patrick showed me just how important they are and how crucial it is that I maintain and defend those standards, whatever life has to throw at me.

My PP normal has allowed me to accept that I am an opinionated old bastard who will not tolerate unfairness, injustice or stupidity. Whilst this has always been a prominent trait within me, the PP me is far more accepting of these characteristics and content to allow them to manifest themselves publicly whenever necessary and appropriate. Impatience and intolerance are now emotions that Patrick has given me the freedom to respond to. No longer harnessed by perceived social pressure to behave in a certain way, and whilst always ensuring my actions are the correct side of the morally acceptable line, and of course legally appropriate, I now go from zero to East London in the blink of an eye. From Phil Schofield to Phil Mitchell quicker than you can say 'Get ou' my pub!'

Patrick taught me that suppressing feelings of injustice, unfairness and frustration are not healthy and that they need to be addressed.

My ex-wife once told a professional with whom we were working, and whose inadequacies were causing some angst, 'I know he comes across as a nice guy, and he is a nice guy, but you really don't want to piss him off.'

It was very sound advice and something that those who have wronged me since will wish they had known before they decided to deal with me in an improper and unjust way. Patrick has left me with a belief, although not necessarily the socially acceptable view, that revenge is very sweet.

Following my dismissal from my job, Patrick, at least for a while, wallowed in his smug enjoyment of the unforeseen misery the unfairness had created for me. The subsequent lies that were allowed to spread amongst the school community and beyond further added to the suffering. Lies that it was impossible for me to address, and which continue to cause me issues both personally and professionally.

Eventually though even Patrick had to accept the injustice of it all.

One evening as we sat together on my sofa his usual air of sarcasm and superciliousness was replaced by a far more empathetic almost caring tone as he said, 'You know, Fry, as Valery Legasov once said, "Every lie incurs a debt to the truth. Sooner or later that debt must be paid."

Patrick and Legasov were right, and I am now very sure that all such debts owing to me will eventually be paid.

EPILOGUE

Journey's End

I did it. Patrick appeared out of nowhere and forced me to endure, for what seemed like an eternity, the most dysfunctional, toxic, damaging relationship. He hurt me, bullied me, taunted and embarrassed me, but I got through it. I eventually managed to shake him off. My relationship with Patrick is now simply a chapter in the book of my life.

Like all relationships and experiences, my adventures with Patrick have shaped me as a person. I am, most definitely, a different Ian Fry to the one I was before I met Patrick and, perhaps surprisingly, the changes are almost exclusively positive ones. Positive for me, my children and Liss, but very much a negative for those who might think it is a good idea to treat either me or my family with anything other than transparency, fairness and honesty.

My adventures with Patrick may be over, but those of the Family Fry, now including Liss, are most definitely not. I will never forget my time with my little furry friend and the adventures we had together. As a travel companion he was pretty shit, and it was not an experience I would want to repeat. Although my Trip Advisor assessment would be pretty damning, it certainly ranks top of my list of influential, extraordinary, once (hopefully) in a lifetime experiences.

Like any significant relationship we had our ups and downs. It was certainly tumultuous and extremely hard work. Patrick was generally pretty fucking hideous and an utter shit to live with. Together we redefined 'toxic relationship', for toxic it most certainly was, in every conceivable sense.

We are all the product of our past. Patrick is now, thankfully, part of mine, but like all our life experiences, both good and bad, he has shaped me into the person I now am and provided me with a new, fresher, more positive outlook on life, my life.

Now, though, that relationship and the adventures of me and Patrick are over. I have finally rid myself of the parasitic, merciless, destructive leech that ruled my life for so long. Our double act has been consigned to my dustbin of human experience, and whilst the odour of our rotting association lingers in the air, he is gone, never to be seen again, hopefully.

ACKNOWLEDGEMENTS

I had always imagined writing to be a relatively insular process and in many ways it is. However, I must acknowledge that this book would never have happened were it not for a number of very special people. Even more importantly I would not have been around to write it at all but for the kindness, friendship and/or expertise of an additional few.

As an author I have to thank all those who helped me to transform an idea and some random notes in a journal into a manuscript. My friend, Sara Downing, herself an author, who had the misfortune to read my very first draft and was kind enough not to scoff at my initial pathetic attempts at writing but instead gave me the belief that those original ramblings could become something more, as well as providing many invaluable notes. Emer McCarthy, my fantastically honest friend, who was also kind enough to read through early drafts and provide valuable feedback.

Without the expertise, input and support of the wonderful Michelle Emerson (publishing guru) it is likely my adventures with Patrick would have never seen the light of day. My editors Sarah Healy (who edited an early version of my manuscript) and Kimberley Miller have been amazingly kind and supportive.

My wonderful wife, Melissa, has endured hour upon hour of me writing, re-writing and writing again this book without (much) complaint.

As someone who lives with severe clinical depression I know I would not be here were it not for the friendship of Damon Norville who had the very dubious honour of being my closest friend during one of the worst periods of my life. The wonderful team of psychiatric nurses, psychiatrists and psychologists who saw me through the breakdowns, and continue to help me, with their advice, support and no small amount of medication.

For the me who ventured out on this journey with Patrick I have to thank the fantastic medical professionals at Worcester Royal Hospital. My consultants Mr Christopher Ayshford (ENT) and Dr Fiona Clark (Haemotology) without whose expertise it is no exaggeration to say I would not be alive today. The nurses and staff of Rowan Suite endured my company for six long months during the summer and autumn of my adventures with Patrick. They were saintly in their patience and care and had it not all been so shit it would have been almost enjoyable thanks to this group of magnificent human beings.

MacMillan provided fantastic support to me before, during and after my treatment.

Most importantly I must acknowledge the part played by my beautiful children – Mollie, Elizabeth and

William. Their unintentional contributions to my journey with Patrick helped to keep me (relatively) sane and were an added bonus to their existing and continuous most significant contribution to my life – just being them.

NOTES

2. PATRICK

1. Siddhartha Mukharjee 'The Emperor of all Maladies, a Biography of Cancer' (2010)

3. A JOURNEY NOT A BATTLE

1. Christopher Hitchens *Mortality* (2012)
2. Jess Tardy – Twitter (2017)
3. Lisa Lynch *The C Word* (2010)

10. I HATE LOSING

1. UKGov poll (Macmillan Cancer Support) (2019)
2. Mukharjee

KEEP IN TOUCH!

Email – ianfry30@yahoo.co.uk
Twitter – @meandpatrick

Printed in Great Britain
by Amazon